RAW
CAKE

Beautiful, nutritious and indulgent raw
sweets, treats, cakes and elixirs

RAW CAKE

Daisy Kristiansen
Leah Garwood-Gowers
of **THE HARDIHOOD**

bluebird
books for life

First published 2017 by Bluebird
an imprint of Pan Macmillan
20 New Wharf Road, London N1 9RR
Associated companies throughout the world
www.panmacmillan.com

ISBN 978-1-5098-2865-4

Publisher Carole Tonkinson
Project Editor Laura Nickoll
Art Direction & Design Charlotte Heal Design
Photography Lizzie Mayson
Prop Styling Jemima Hetherington

Visit www.panmacmillan.com to read more about all our books and to buy them.
You will also find features, author interviews and news of any author events, and
you can sign up for e-newsletters so that you're always first to hear about our new releases.

Please note that the advice in this book is for general information only, and should not be taken as a substitute for qualified
medical advice. If you have a medical condition, are pregnant, or suffer from allergies, please consult your doctor before
changing your diet or taking supplements, Chinese medicines or herbal remedies. Bee pollen can provoke a severe reaction
if you have a pollen allergy. Avoid if pregnant or breastfeeding, or if you are taking blood-thinning medication.

CONTENTS

Introduction

This book is for those new to raw food, the experimental and those who are simply excited about getting more nourishment from their sweet treats.

Back in 2014, when we made our first raw chocolate brownies, we were absolute beginners – all we knew was that we wanted to make beautiful desserts using nothing but natural ingredients. The only rule we had was that raw cake by The Hardihood had to be abundant and flavoursome and never bland or boring. Through a lot of trial, error and spilt nut milk, we got to grips first with the basics and then with the complexities of raw dessert-making.

Since then, The Hardihood has become known for its crisp, minimal, luxurious aesthetic. Here we want to share with you how we created our products, our journey, and the tips and techniques that we've picked up along the way. Forget everything you thought you knew about making cakes without butter, eggs and flour – we're here to give raw a good name! Here we'll share our collection of recipes for raw cheesecake, chocolate indulgences, ice creams, pudding pots, breakfast bowls, smoothies, tonics and superfood blends.

Like a lot of things in life our most brilliant breakthroughs have been born from the ashes of disaster. We've had a lot of fun, though, and we try not to take cake-making too seriously. It's this light-heartedness that we want to pass on to you. Don't be afraid of failure. You're working with delicious, wholesome ingredients; however it looks in the end, we promise it'll taste great. Relax and enjoy it – everything tastes better when served with a smile.

Our Story

We've been friends for nearly a decade, during most of which we lived together in an East London warehouse, back when rent was cheap. We met at a fancy dinner party that we'd both been persuaded to go to and it wasn't long before we realized that we were the only ones at the table giggling at each other's jokes. We took the long bus ride home to Hackney together and haven't stopped laughing since.

We didn't know, at first, that we were destined for a life of raw cake. Before dreaming up The Hardihood we worked in fashion and in lifestyle journalism. Like any self-respecting city dwellers, we were passionate about London's diverse food scene; we'd try somewhere new every week and delight in sharing our findings. Getting to know London through its best-loved dining spots, we looked for innovative menus, fresh food and good vibes.

Soon we began to notice a rise in LA-inspired cold-press juice bars and Sydney-style cafés with a focus on wellness, and as our curiosity prompted us to travel around London for a taste of the good life, our intrigue grew with each feel-good food spot that we visited. The more far-out the dish, the more inspired we were; nut milk, matcha lattes, chia seeds, raw cacao – it was all new to us and we loved it. We discovered ayurveda, healing foods, holistic health and raw cuisine, sampled medicinal mushrooms, fermented vegetables, powdered roots and drank charcoal infusions. We felt like the world was onto something; people were beginning to look at food in a different way, rejoicing in getting their five-a-day instead of being burdened by it. Accompanied by our new year's resolution to give up refined sugar, this felt like an awakening. We became immersed in the idea of wellness and wondered why our local neighbourhood didn't have more to offer. Growing tired of the trek across town, we decided to experiment with our own creations instead. We bought a food processor, a shed-load of dates, nuts and coconut oil and got to work.

Looking back now, we laugh at our first attempts to master raw desserts – our trials mostly included chucking everything into a blender and hoping for the best. There were soggy cheesecakes, droopy brownies and crumbly flapjacks, but miraculously, we weren't deterred. We loved this new approach to baking and were as excited about the journey as we were about the destination.

In the early days we formulated creations from our kitchens at home, as although we no longer lived together our houses were a five-minute walk away. We'd spend all of our spare time trying out new recipes, sourcing ingredients and reading up on techniques. We bought the books and became friendly with our local greengrocers so that they'd let us purchase in bulk. We tested everything we made on our male friends as well as female, because we knew that when it came to cake they wouldn't really care that something was good for them, we knew they'd just give it to us straight. We were adamant that our cakes would always be absurdly delicious, not just a 'free-from' alternative.

Because our creations are so visual we documented the whole thing on Instagram from the start; we learned how to style the cakes and became enthralled with kitchenware, ceramics, tea towels – you name it. We built up a repertoire of recipes that we were proud of and began to receive orders, first from our friends, then from people who'd heard about us through word of mouth or online. As the weeks went by we'd make an increasing number of cakes, getting more adventurous with each order.

In the winter of 2015 we were invited to sell cakes at Paris Fashion Week. We were delighted and agreed immediately, thinking we'd figure out the logistics later. In the end we took the Eurostar with seven suitcases and the help of Daisy's husband. We had our ingredients delivered to a depot on the outskirts of Paris and used Airbnb to transform someone's kitchen into a production unit. It was probably one of our most brilliantly ridiculous adventures to date, topped only by returning the following year by car and doing the same thing all over again. Introducing the international fashion crowd to raw cake was transformational and we've worked hand in hand with the fashion industry ever since.

We outgrew our home kitchens pretty quickly and soon began looking for something more functional. Our only prerequisites were that the space would have good natural light and plenty of room for fridges, but aside from that we were happy to have any space that we could call our own. As it happens, we got lucky, really lucky, and we moved into a studio in the centre of the area we had set out to transform. We have a skylight, exposed beams and a garden and we definitely know how good we've got it.

Signing the lease on our own studio kitchen was pivotal. We were able to dedicate all of our time to our passion, filling the cupboards with all sorts of superfoods, herbs and tinctures. We hired our first employee and became a tiny team of three, learning a little bit more each day about creating beautiful desserts using natural, raw ingredients.

7

Why Raw?

It was through our commitment to find a way to make delicious desserts that were free from refined sugar and processed ingredients that we discovered raw cuisine, a plant-based style of preparing food in which components aren't heated above a certain temperature. The exact temperature is disputed, with some saying 40°C and others saying 49°C. We settle for around 42°C.

We love raw desserts because the ingredients we use are naturally free from refined sugar, gluten, dairy and soy, and are worlds away from processed 'free-from' foods, which are often loaded with substitutes to replace whichever food group they're trying to avoid (and aren't necessarily healthier). We love pushing the limits of raw, natural, superfood ingredients to create the best possible confectionery, in every way. And there's no denying that we feel great on it.

First, though, we want to be clear. Neither of us eats an entirely raw diet. London is often chilly and we wake up craving a hot bowl of porridge or soup. Really, it's about listening to your body and doing what feels best for it based on the information that you have. The cravings we used to have for pick 'n' mix and Ben & Jerry's now feel more like cravings for raw Snickers bars or our Salted Caramel Crunch Bars. As our consciousness around food shifted, so did our cravings. It's all part of a learning process and a journey that is to be enjoyed.

The Hardihood Philosophy

The Hardihood philosophy is simple; we believe that people should have complete freedom of choice when it comes to what they're putting into their bodies and shouldn't have to compromise on flavour or decadence in doing so. We're foodies at heart, and because of this our Raw Cake creations will always be every bit as delicious as the desserts you grew up with, only with the added benefit of nutritious ingredients. This lifestyle is most definitely not about going without; it's about embracing what makes your body feel good, what makes you happy and the numerous ways you can have your cake and eat it.

Sharing our journey with you feels like a natural getting together with friends. We don't want to keep our discoveries to ourselves, we want to get out there and share the good vibes! We live in a world where it's easier to meaningfully connect to the internet than each other – now more than ever we need to make a conscious effort to treat people right in real time and eat real food while we're at it.

Modern Alchemy

Like most people, we grew up trying to believe in magic: *The Craft*, *Hocus Pocus*, *The Worst Witch*, *Charmed*... Of course, the rational brain knew it all along, but there was still a part of us that cried when we realized we would never receive a letter of acceptance from Hogwarts. The next few years were spent mainly forgetting about enchantment and learning how to become grown-ups. Believing in Flower Fairies and casting spells over garden-foraged potions of pinecones, pebbles and vacant snail shells faded like distant memories. It wasn't until later that we rediscovered alchemy – in the form of healing herbs, elixirs and tonics. We've learned to balance our bodies' needs by supplementing our diets with herbs and superfoods that add flavour, colour, depth and healing to our meals. It's fascinating.

By using natural ingredients and ancient wisdom, we support the chemistry of the human

8

body while having fun and creating beautiful food. These days it's easy to grab a bag of spirulina or maca from your local supermarket, and for the more unusual ingredients we usually head to a health food shop or the internet. Trust us, though, the hunt for the obscure is all part of the enjoyment; we were like kids in a candy shop when we got to run wild in LA for a week, buying up all of the powders, pills and pastilles we'd heard of and those we'd not heard of!

Getting Started

If this is your first foray into the world of raw, don't be nervous – we were you not so long ago. One of the great things about raw baking is its simplicity. Unlike traditional baking, it's not an exact science, so it leaves plenty of room for creativity and constructive failure. We find working with wholesome natural ingredients rewarding because they're so pure. You know exactly what you're going to get out of a recipe because you know exactly what you put into it. Working with foods that only have the name of one ingredient listed on the back of the packaging is liberating.

Feel Free to Experiment

There are many ways to expand on the recipes in this book and there are many ways to simplify them. When we first began reading raw recipe books we were bewildered by how complicated they were and the length of the ingredient lists. We began to excel at improvization and we urge you to improvize, too. If you're about to start preparing your dessert and suddenly realize you don't have enough of something in stock, experiment by substituting it with something similar. The same can be said for superfood powders – if you don't have a specific ingredient

in your cupboard already or you're waiting for it to arrive after ordering it online (this happens to us all the time), don't be afraid to use something else. There are no rules here and, who knows, you might find a variation that works better for you this way.

You can simplify this even more by making your own ingredients if you have the time. There's something very satisfying about seeing the ingredients in one form one minute and then minutes later they're setting in the fridge, unaltered, only presented differently.

Back to the Future

Eating as organically as possible allows us to return to our roots and to how our great grandparents ate. It is also a great way to connect to nature if you are living in a busy city. Of course, eating home-grown or organic produce is not only good for our bodies but also for the environment. Minimizing pesticides, synthetic fertilizers, hormones and antibiotics means that the produce is fresher and less toxic. Organic farming methods reduce soil and water contamination, help preserve local wildlife, encourage biodiversity and are generally more sustainable.

Inspiration and Influence

Travel is the source of inspiration that we tap into repeatedly when we are coming up with ideas for The Hardihood. It was upon returning from respective trips to Japan and Ibiza that The Hardihood was initially founded, and we revisit our mental scrap-books regularly.

Ibiza

Leah has family in Ibiza and over the years has spent many joyful summers frolicking in the rural beauty of the island. Rising with the

9

sun became a tradition for us in Ibiza and when we explored the island together we'd drive down dust-covered tracks to a different cove each morning, capturing the light on camera before dipping into the ocean and swimming in whichever direction the tide took us. Once we'd had enough we'd clamber onto the rocks and soak up the morning rays, only half watching as the sun turned our soggy footprints to ghosts.

To a backdrop of Bohemian campsites, jagged cliff edges and dramatic coastlines, Leah grew up experiencing the serenity of the wilderness, its vastness disrupted only by wildlife and the sound of the wind. It's this connection to nature that we focus on when we need to cultivate a little space in our excitable city lives; a peaceful sensation to call upon when life picks up pace.

Copenhagen

For Daisy, marrying a Dane has meant making Copenhagen her second home. Like the calm water that runs through the city to the wild, windswept beaches, there's a settled sense of serenity in this sleepy toy-town. Breathing in the crisp air as you plod along the winding canals you realize that there's no reason to move any faster. Here, nothing is rushed; architecture, design, life, it's all carried out with the same considered precision. Scandinavian minimalism is no accident.

Scavenger bike rides to the summerhouse allotment to forage for wild rosehips, fresh blueberries, gooseberries, blackberries, lemon balm and stevia interweave the city with nature seamlessly. Evening meals are put together using the day's finds and are relished with friends and family. The Danish word 'Hygge' describes this heart-warming energy, and although there isn't a direct translation we see it simply as the Danish ritual of enjoying life's simple pleasures. Time spent with loved ones is savoured, and creating a beautiful environment in which to share moments is an important part of this.

Japan

A visual rollercoaster of bright lights and colours you've never seen before, there's nowhere in the world that pushes you as deliciously close to sensory overload as Japan. A rocket ride into the world of the unknown, every moment is experienced in high definition. If our minds had memory cards they'd have been full in a heartbeat. Every unknown food has to be tasted, every texture touched, every graphic store-front admired and every oddity recorded. Mouth open in awe is how we took in Tokyo.

It was Daisy's 2014 trip here that ignited a feverous passion for packaging, a penchant for the well-presented. Without understanding a word of the language, Japanese branding speaks loud and clear. No opportunity to exhibit excellence is wasted; even tea leaves are wrapped to perfection. In the largest city in the world, where it feels like somebody hit fast forward, time stands still when it comes to tradition.

Los Angeles

We touched down on Californian turf after 11 hours of excited squirming on a tightly packed British Airways flight. We'd booked the trip to our dream destination on a whim and given ourselves a week in which to satisfy our expectations. The balmy coastal warmth welcomed us from the airport, the sky was clear and we winked at the moon and the stars in the magic of the moment.

When we woke the next morning our neighbourhood was full of single-storey buildings and the views were stretching way out into the horizon. Palm trees towered over Silver Lake as the sun rose over the city. We were surrounded by space and our eyes revelled in remembering how to use the full range of their vision as we looked into the distance. Urban cacti and succulents grew freely in the streets and punctuated our stroll to a yoga class that morning. The mismatched houses and villas existed without correlation, an endless spectrum of colours and shades. The light broke through the branches of botanical plants, casting our giddy shadows in the Californian light.

We ventured to our local Moon Juice where we met Jeremy, our dear friend and seasoned LA tour guide, before driving top-down in his Mustang to visit a food show in Anaheim as palm tree silhouettes dusted the sky. Even before we visited the Rose Bowl Flea Market, House of Intuition and Café Gratitude, we knew that we were madly, truly, deeply in love with the wild, wild West Coast.

London

London is home; it's the city in which we dreamt up The Hardihood over two cups of tea on a cold evening in January. It's under this skyline that we went on mad hunts for mesquite; ran a tab with our local organic shop to fund our first recipe trials; discovered raw chocolate and the uplifting benefits of cacao, a million miles from the ancient civilizations of South America. The city we live in has become our inspiration, our teacher and our motivation.

From the age-old establishments that have been going against the grain since day dot, committed to keeping it organic before people were prepared to pay more for it, to the innovative start-ups that have risked it all to bring a new perspective to the market as well as those who are simply courageous enough to try something new; you're the reason why we love this city, we know you'll always keep us on our toes, reaching for the stars.

Energy: An Afterword

The Hardihood began life as a labour of love and we feel grateful every day that it's developed into something that's able to sustain us. We've learned to believe in our creative ability, and we now know that listening to our hearts will seldom take us down the wrong path in the long run. We try to release attachments to outcomes and let progress show up in whatever way it likes, so we can celebrate every breakthrough, no matter what it is.

Investing in our hopes, dreams and longings is as important as investing in our bodies. Take time for yourself, show your friends how much they mean to you and smile at strangers in the street; kindness costs nothing and we try to sprinkle it on everything. We do our best to stay away from envy, jealousy and bad vibes and surround ourselves with the people who inspire us. We have also learned how to say no.

Believe in magic, believe in healing and believe in building the most brilliant life that you could ever imagine for yourself. Stay in your power and trust your gut. Never show up empty handed to a party or closed minded to a conversation, allow yourself to embrace your quiet side and to dance with your inner party animal. You are unique; find your magic and commit to staying there.

13

Equipment

If you want to keep it raw, when it comes to equipment there are a few bits that are essential to kick-start your journey.

If you're only just starting out and you don't have much equipment yet, begin with cheaper models of some kit and then upgrade to something more powerful – and expensive! – as you get The Hardihood Raw Cake bug.

Food Processor

You won't get very far without a food processor, but this doesn't mean that you need to splash out on a really expensive model. Start small like we did and who knows, you might end up with a whole family of whizzing, blending, shredding machines one day.

Essential for fine-chopping nuts, dates and seeds, a food processor breaks down any-thing you put in it and, unlike a blender, it won't conk out without liquid. Again the more high-powered the better, but we got great results from our trusty £60 entry level model for at least the first two years of experimenting, and we're actually far too attached to it so it still sits alongside the super-powerful industrial machines we use now.

Blender

There are many different blenders on the market and our advice is to pretty much avoid the cheaper models and wait until you can afford something more mid-range. You'll need something quite high-speed for getting creams and liquids really smooth.

Dehydrator

Dehydrators vary vastly in quality and in price. In all honesty you don't desperately need one – we didn't have one for a long time, and none of the recipes in this book require one – but if you're lucky enough to have space in your kitchen for one or happen to have one already, consider it a blessing. They're a bit of an eye-sore but are great for drying out raw dough or decorative fruit without using too much warmth. If you don't have a dehydrator, you can use your oven on its lowest heat setting for a longer period of time, although dehydrators are much more economically and environmentally friendly than leaving your oven on.

14

Pre-cake Prep

Soaking Nuts

Activating nuts basically just involves soaking them overnight to remove the phytates and enzyme inhibitors that surround them to protect them from predators or sprouting too early. Not only are soaked nuts smoother and creamier when blended but they're prepared in a way that grants our bodies access to the full range of nutritional benefits without the worry of gut irritation. Do this by measuring out the quantity of nuts that you need before adding them to a jar or container and covering them with cool filtered water and leaving overnight. If you need to speed up the process, use warm water and cover for a few hours, checking periodically to see if they're ready. You're looking for a spongy absorbent consistency. Be sure to drain the water and give the nuts a rinse before either letting them dry in the dehydrator or oven, or use them while wet.

Soaking Dates

We often find that no two bags of dates are the same: some are soft and gooey while others are rock solid. To soften dates, and make them stickier, we soak them in two ways: either in cold filtered water overnight or in warm water for a few hours. Sometimes you'll want a soft and runny consistency like a syrup, if you're using them in a smoothie or a sauce, but at other times the recipe will call for a firmer, tacky consistency, if they are to be used as a binding agent in a base. Use your judgement as to whether dates are soft enough; it'll depend on a few factors: how powerful your blender is, the desired consistency of the mixture, and which dates you're using. Medjool dates rarely need soaking for long, unless you're looking to achieve a syrupy or liquid consistency.

Melting Coconut Oil

Coconut oil is hugely versatile. It can be used solid at room temperature or cooler, and as a liquid when heated. We use a lot of liquid coconut oil because pouring it into cups minimizes wastage and is much easier and faster to work with. In order to melt the coconut oil, we pour lukewarm water into a container and place the jar of coconut oil in it with the lid on, ensuring that none of the water gets into the oil. Once it has turned to liquid we use it straight away or within the next half hour to make sure it doesn't re-set.

Chapter 1

Making your own ingredients is a great place to start if you've just begun your journey into raw. These simple recipes are not only the building blocks for a lot of the desserts that we make, but also for our day-to-day lives. Although it's easier to find really good-quality nut butters and nut milks in the shops these days, we always keep a few jars of homemade nut milk in the fridge and nut butters on the shelf, and our friends have even been known to receive them as gifts on special occasions. One of the keys to making your own is never throwing away your empty jars – wash them thoroughly and put them away; that way you'll always have something to store your creations in.

Nut & Seed Butters

Nuts and seeds can be a fantastic source of energy, some B vitamins, vitamin E, zinc, iron, manganese, potassium, magnesium, calcium, fibre, protein, and they have the added bonus of containing antioxidants and essential fatty acids. Flax seeds, hemp seeds and walnuts are the best options if you're looking for omega-3 fats. Nuts and seeds are the perfect snack to help lower cholesterol, though do be aware they are pretty high in calories because of all those healthy fats.

However, although nuts and seeds are considered to be a healthy option, we cannot absorb their beneficial nutrients fully without first soaking them. This is because raw nuts contain enzyme inhibitors and phytates that naturally protect them until proper growing conditions occur, ensuring that the nut or seed will not sprout prematurely.

Soaking them is a simple process. Place the nuts in a medium-large bowl and cover with cold filtered water. Leave the bowl in a cool, shaded place covered with a clean tea towel (see soaking times in the box on the left), and then once the required time is up, drain the nuts, discard the water, rinse the nuts in fresh running water and drain again.

Leave the nuts to dry off, then dehydrate them in a dehydrator – if you have one – or, alternatively, use your oven, set no higher than 42°C or at its lowest setting. Spread the nuts out evenly on a baking tray and place in the oven for 12–16 hours, turning the nuts occasionally to make sure they are drying evenly.

19

Soaking Times

There are differing views as to how long each type of nut or seed needs to be soaked for, depending on the particular variety and as a result of their different levels of absorbency and minerals, but this is what works for us:

Almonds	8–10 hours
Brazil nuts	None
Cashews	2 hours
Flax seeds	8 hours
Hazelnuts	8 hours
Hemp seeds	None
Macadamias	8 hours
Peanuts	8–10 hours
Pecans	6 hours
Pine nuts	8 hours
Pistachios	None
Pumpkin seeds	6 hours
Sesame seeds	6–8 hours
Sunflower seeds	2 hours
Walnuts	6 hours

How to Make Nut & Seed Butters

Maca almond butter
290g (2 cups) almonds,
    soaked for 8–10 hours
    and dehydrated
1 tbsp maca powder
2 tbsp coconut sugar
2 tbsp coconut oil, melted
pinch of Himalayan salt

Baobab peanut butter
300g (2 cups) peanuts,
    soaked for 8–10 hours
    and dehydrated
1 tbsp baobab powder
2 tbsp coconut sugar
2 tbsp coconut oil, melted
pinch of Himalayan salt

Cashew cinnamon butter
260g (2 cups) cashews,
    soaked for 2 hours
    and dehydrated
2 tsp ground cinnamon
2 tbsp coconut sugar
3 tbsp coconut oil, melted
pinch of Himalayan salt

First, decide on any flavourings you might want to include, such as dates, vanilla powder, ground cinnamon, grated nutmeg, coconut sugar, maple syrup, ground ginger, turmeric, cacao, maca, lucuma or chaga powders or coconut nectar, etc. Choose your favourites and be creative! We've listed the ingredients for our top three favourite nut butters on the left.

Once you've decided on your nuts or seeds and flavours, place the quantity of your chosen nuts in your food processor (see *TIP*) and blend on high until they break down to a powder, then stop and scrape down the sides as many times as necessary to work the mixture back in. Keep processing for a further 10 minutes, then pour in the melted coconut oil. If you don't love the taste of coconut oil, try a 'cuisine' oil – a flavourless version.

Continue blending for a further 5–10 minutes until the butter becomes smooth and creamy. This can take a while longer depending on your machine, but keep on going even if you think it's not working!

Sprinkle in a pinch of high-quality salt at the end, as this brings out the sweet flavours of the nuts or seeds and gives the butter a richer, more balanced taste.

TIP: Using a high-powered processor will help a lot when making nut butters, as you need a strong motor that will not conk out over the longer blending times! We use a Magimix, Robot Coupe or a Sage blender – all of which are fantastic.

Nut Milks

Nut milks are an invaluable addition to any fridge – they're a dairy-free alternative with benefits. We drink them in the morning for a nutrient-rich, plant-based protein boost or in the evening blended with ginger and ashwagandha for a soothing bedtime tipple. We also use them in cakes, puddings and smoothies.

Just as for nut butters (see pages 19–20), soaking nuts before blending them to use in milks is important, not just for preserving their nutritional benefits and making them easier to digest, but also because it helps with the blending stage itself – fully soaked nuts blend more smoothly and leave less pulp behind.

How to Make Nut Milks

Place the nuts in a medium-large bowl and cover with cold filtered water, adding a pinch of Himalayan salt. Leave the bowl in a cool, shaded place, covered with a clean tea towel (see soaking times on page 19), then once the required time is up, drain the nuts, discard the water, rinse the nuts under fresh running water and drain again.

21

Blend with fresh filtered water in a high-powered blender on high at a ratio of 4 parts water to 1 part nuts. At this stage, add in any extra flavourings that you'd like.

Pour the blended liquid through a nut milk bag into a large bowl or jug for a smooth texture and discard the pulp.

If you want to save money on ingredients and curb the high price tag of homemade nut milks, replace half the nuts with soaked brown rice.

Strawberry
& Almond Milk

215g (1½ cups) raw almonds,
  soaked for 8-10 hours
1 litre (4 cups) filtered water
290g (2 cups) strawberries
2 tbsp acai powder
1 tbsp coconut syrup or
  alternative liquid natural
  sweetener
½ tsp vanilla powder
pinch of Himalayan salt

Drain the almonds and rinse in fresh water. Blend on high in a high-powered blender with the water. Add the strawberries, acai powder, sweetener, vanilla and salt and pulse again for 1–2 minutes.

Pour through a nut milk bag into a large bowl or measuring jug, discard the pulp, and store the nut milk in a clean, sealed bottle in the fridge for 2–3 days.

Cashew
& Maca Milk

22

130g (1 cup) cashews,
  soaked for 2 hours
1 litre (4 cups) filtered water
3 pitted Medjool dates
½ tsp vanilla powder
1 tbsp maca powder
pinch of Himalayan salt

Drain the cashews and rinse in fresh water. Blend on high in a high-powered blender with the water. Add the dates, vanilla, maca and salt and pulse again for 1–2 minutes.

Pour through a nut milk bag into a large bowl or measuring jug, discard the pulp, and store the nut milk in a clean, sealed bottle in the fridge for 2–3 days.

Above: Strawberry & Almond Milk

making your own ingredients

Date & Hemp Seed Milk

110g (1 cup) shelled hemp seeds
1 litre (4 cups) filtered water
5 pitted Medjool dates
pinch of Himalayan salt

Hemp seeds do not need soaking, so this is a quick and easy recipe with no prep time. Blend all the ingredients in a high-powered blender on high for 1–2 minutes until smooth.

Pour through a nut milk bag into a large bowl or measuring jug, discard the pulp, and store the seed milk in a clean, sealed bottle in the fridge for 2–3 days.

Pistachio & Cinnamon Milk

100g (1 cup) pistachios
1 litre (4 cups) filtered water
2 tbsp coconut syrup or
    alternative liquid natural
    sweetener
½ tbsp ground cinnamon
pinch of Himalayan salt

Pistachios do not require soaking before using, so just blend all the ingredients in a high-powered blender on high for 1–2 minutes until smooth.

Pour through a nut milk bag into a large bowl or measuring jug, discard the pulp, and store the nut milk in a clean, sealed bottle in the fridge for up to 3 days.

Hazelnut & Cacao Milk

125g (1 cup) hazelnuts,
    soaked for 8 hours
1 litre (4 cups) filtered water
2 tbsp cacao powder
2 tbsp maple syrup or
    coconut syrup
½ tsp vanilla powder
pinch of Himalayan salt

Drain the hazelnuts and rinse in fresh water. Blend in a high-powered blender with all the other ingredients on high for 1–2 minutes until smooth.

Pour through a nut milk bag into a large bowl or measuring jug, discard the pulp, and store the nut milk in a clean, sealed bottle in the fridge for up to 3 days.

Above: Pistachio & Cinnamon Milk

making your own ingredients

Date
Paste

Date paste is tricky to get hold of. We've stumbled upon it for sale once from a renowned Turkish restaurateur; it was delicious, but it's just as easy to make your own.

Date paste is one of those things you can't believe is made from just one ingredient. It looks, tastes and behaves just like the caramel that we know and love – only it's better for you.

The best dates to use are the soft Medjool dates, as this large variety has a sumptuous, caramel-like flavour. If you can't get your hands on those, soaking other types of date until they are softer will work just as well.

250g (2 cups) pitted dates
1–2 tbsp water or coconut oil
 (optional)
pinch of Himalayan salt

SERVES 1

Blend the dates in a high-powered food processor on high, stopping to scrape the sides down a few times, then blend for a couple more minutes until a paste starts to form. If you are finding that they're not blending to a smooth paste, add 1–2 tablespoons of water or coconut oil to help them along. Add the salt for a well-rounded, rich, sweet flavour and pulse briefly to combine.

Raw
Chocolate

When you don't have the time to temper your chocolate or go fully fledged chocolatier, this is a simplified raw chocolate recipe that is really easy to whip up in a minute or two. It's not stable enough to be an ingredient for chocolate bars, but it's perfect for decorating your desserts with, pouring over ice cream or smothering your raw pancakes in. What's not to love?

150g (¾ cup) coconut oil,
 melted
170g (½ cup) rice malt syrup
 or coconut syrup
60g (¾ cup) cacao powder

SERVES 1

Blend all the ingredients together in a high-powered food processor on high for a few seconds until well combined – taking care not to over-mix it. Et voila!

raw cake

Above: Raw Chocolate

making your own ingredients

Raw Breakfasts

Chapter 2

A fresh hit of nutrients first thing in the morning is a great way to start the day, best foot forwards. Sometimes we're up and at them in five minutes flat and sometimes we're easy like Sunday morning, but either way we like to enjoy our breakfast. Juices and tonics are great if you wake up feeling like you need some refreshment after a late night; we often stumble into the kitchen and whizz up one of these with our eyes still half closed. Show yourself, your family, your housemate or your guests that you care by whipping up something as the sun comes up.

Chocolate Clean Shake

Think the thick, gloopy chocolate milkshakes of your youth infused with the feel-good benefits of your future. Drinking this in the morning is like turning up the volume of your finest self. We skip down the street after dosing up on this. (*Pictured on pages 28-29.*)

1 banana

250ml (1 cup) nut milk
  (we used almond)

3 pitted Medjool dates

2 tbsp cacao powder

sprinkle of ground cinnamon

pinch of Himalayan salt

1 tbsp reishi powder (optional)

1 tbsp coconut sugar or other
  natural sweetener (optional)

SERVES 1—2

Add all the ingredients, except the sweetener, to a high-powered blender and blend on high until completely smooth. Taste, and if you like it a little sweeter, add the coconut sugar or other natural sweetener.

Nutty Cacao Spread

We don't want to say that this is like Nutella, because it's so much better! A perfect raw treat that can be enjoyed spread on toast, rye bread, pancakes or bananas, or simply eaten with a spoon straight from the jar.

125g (1 cup) hazelnuts,
  soaked for 6-8 hours

50g (½ cup) pecans,
  soaked for 6-8 hours

65g (½ cup) cashews,
  soaked for 6-8 hours

255g (¾ cup) coconut syrup

65g (⅓ cup) coconut oil,
  melted

40g (½ cup) cacao powder

½ tsp vanilla powder

2-3 tbsp tepid water

¼ tsp Himalayan salt

SERVES 2

Drain and rinse the soaked nuts under cold running water, drain again, then place in a high-powered food processor and blend on high for 7–8 minutes. Add the rest of the ingredients and keep processing, scraping down the sides occasionally. The mixture will stay coarse and grainy for some time, and you may find that it takes 15–20 minutes, depending on the power of your machine. For an ultra-silky smooth texture, we finish off the spread in a Vitamix for a few minutes.

Keep in a sealed jar in the fridge for up to 5 days.

Breakfast Thyme Strawberry Smoothie

Complementing sweet flavours with savoury herbs is something we love to do; the thyme in this smoothie absolutely sets it apart from the rest. It's a wholesome, well-rounded favourite that we love to kick off the weekend with. We like to dress it with the edible flowers that we grow in the garden, but if you're in a hurry this is a great one to pour into a jar and eat on the move.

4 small thyme sprigs, plus extra
   to garnish (optional)
7–8 strawberries
1 banana, frozen
½ lemon, peeled
squeeze of lime
1 tbsp peanut butter
1 tbsp linseed
2 tbsp almonds
1 tbsp pumpkin seeds
1 small cucumber or
   ½ medium cucumber
1cm piece of fresh root
   ginger, peeled
60–125ml (¼–½ cup) almond
   milk (depending on how runny
   you want your smoothie)
edible flowers, to garnish
   (optional)

SERVES 1—2

Place all the ingredients, except for the flowers, in a high-powered blender and blend on high until smooth, using as much almond milk as you like to get the smoothie to your preferred consistency.

Garnish with extra thyme sprigs and flowers, if using, and serve straight away.

Thyme
A herb from the mint family, aromatic thyme makes for a great addition to smoothies and drinks, and pairs perfectly with fruits, nuts and seeds. It's hardy too, so easy to grow at home: pop a pot on your windowsill and watch it thrive.

32

raw breakfasts

Creamy Green Smoothie

This does exactly what it says on the tin. Using all of the creamiest smoothie ingredients plus the prebiotic qualities of baobab and the optional immunity-boosting qualities of cordyceps (see page 183), this drink will wow everyone who tastes it.

1½ bananas
¾ avocado, stoned
1 tbsp baobab powder
1 tbsp cordyceps (optional)
1 lime, peeled
2 tbsp cashews
large splash of almond milk, plus extra if you like your smoothie runny

SERVES 1—2

Place all the ingredients in a high-powered blender and blend on high until smooth, using as much almond milk as you like to get the smoothie to your preferred consistency.

Mint Green Smoothie

This was inspired by a smoothie we tried in LA. The cacao nibs give it that extra crunch and the rocket takes it up a notch in terms of spice. We like to include rocket in our smoothies and juices because it contains DIM (Dindolylmethane), a great natural hormone balancer and fat breakdown stimulator.

2 bananas
handful of spinach
handful of rocket
splash of almond milk
2 pitted Medjool dates
6 mint sprigs, stalks and all
¼ tsp vanilla powder
1 tbsp cacao nibs
2 tbsp hemp seeds
2 tbsp pumpkin seeds

SERVES 1—2

Place all the ingredients in a high-powered blender and blend on high until smooth and creamy.

raw breakfasts

Spirulina & Apricot Breakfast Bar

Good mornings start with one of these nutritionally packed bars in one hand and a warm drink in the other. These easy bars are packed with goodness and will set you off on your day in fighting form. Keep a batch in the fridge for the week or devour in one swoop.

155g (1 cup) dried apricots

70g (1 cup) gluten-free oats

2 tbsp chia seed

40g (¼ cup) golden linseed

2 tbsp hemp seeds

70g (½ cup) pumpkin seeds

55g (½ cup) goji berries

85g (¼ cup) date syrup
   or maple syrup

80g (⅓ cup) almond butter

1½ tbsp spirulina

pinch of Himalayan salt

MAKES 6–8 BARS

Line a shallow 15cm square baking tin with baking paper.

Place the apricots in a high-powered food processor and pulse until roughly broken up. Add the oats, seeds and goji berries and pulse again a few more times to combine everything.

Transfer the seed mixture to a bowl and pour in the syrup, almond butter and spirulina, then add the salt. Mix together by hand, making sure the seed mixture is evenly coated with the almond butter and syrup.

Press the mixture into the baking tin and refrigerate for 3–4 hours or overnight before cutting into 6–8 chunky bars. Store in the fridge for up to 1 week.

36

Spirulina
A brilliant source of plant protein, several B vitamins and iron, spirulina boosts this breakfast bar's credentials no end. Buy organic spirulina if you can get hold of it.

raw breakfasts

raw cake

Apple & Ginger Chia Seed Pudding

Chia seeds are such a versatile blessing. As they're known for their energy-giving abilities, it makes sense to begin the day with them. The addition of ginger to this scrumptious pudding gives it an extra kick and will assist in the smooth digestion of meals.

1 apple, cored, plus extra,
   thinly sliced, to serve
1cm piece of fresh ginger,
   peeled and chopped
190ml (¾ cup) nut milk
35g (¼ cup) chia seeds
1 tbsp maple syrup
coconut yoghurt, to serve

SERVES 1

Blend the apple with the ginger, nut milk and maple syrup in a high-powered blender on high until completely smooth.

Pour into a bowl and add the chia seeds, mixing them in with a spoon until well combined, then place in the fridge for 30 minutes–1 hour until the chia seeds have expanded and the mixture is gel-like. Spoon over the coconut yoghurt, garnish with extra sliced apple and serve immediately.

39

Red Root Savoury Smoothie

When we've eaten cake all day, there are times when we just crave something light and savoury. Love at first sip, this is a great source of antioxidants and anti-inflammatory ingredients; breakfast, lunch or dinner, this fragrant blend is reminiscent of a creamy take on gazpacho.

½ raw beetroot

4 medium-sized vine tomatoes
    or 8 small plum tomatoes

½ carrot

1cm piece of fresh root
    ginger, peeled

1cm piece of fresh turmeric
    root, peeled

½ medium hot chilli
    pepper, seeds in

30g (¼ cup) macadamias

60ml (¼ cup) almond milk

250ml (1 cup) filtered water

ice cubes (optional)

SERVES 1–2

Make sure the beetroot, tomatoes and carrot are washed thoroughly. Blend all the ingredients except the ice cubes in a high-powered blender on high for 2–3 minutes until smooth.

Serve immediately, with some ice cubes if you like, for a fresh, chilled smoothie.

Raw Beetroot

Beetroot is a brilliant liver cleanser. The liver is responsible for filtering the blood and is one of your front line defences against harmful toxins and chemicals. Given this heavy workload, it's good to take care of your liver when you can by consuming liver-function-boosting foods.

raw breakfasts

raw cake

Mango & Macadamia Smoothie

Mangos are so uplifting, they're believed to clear the skin and refresh the body from the inside out. This smoothie is literally happiness in a glass; we'll drink it any time of day if we're feeling a little bit low and want something indulgent but light.

1 medium-large mango, peeled, destoned and chopped

1 banana

65g (½ cup) macadamias

250ml (1 cup) almond or other nut milk

1 tbsp hemp or pea protein powder

¼ tbsp vanilla powder

SERVES 1–2

Blend all the ingredients together in a high-powered blender on high until smooth. If you prefer a runnier smoothie, add a dash of water. Serve immediately.

43

Macadamia Nuts
Rich in monounsaturated fatty acids, creamy macadamia nuts have a waxy texture and a buttery taste, making them perfectly suited to raw desserts and indulgent smoothies.

Berry & Schisandra Bowl

If you wake up feeling foggy, this zingy bowl can really cut through the mist. Berries are generally rich in antioxidants, while schisandra is known for being a bit of a beauty tonic as it's thought to protect the skin from sun and wind exposure, allergic reactions and environmental stress. Eat this if you want to be wide awake and looking fine.

288g (2 cups) mixed berries
   (we used strawberries,
   raspberries, blueberries)
190ml (¾ cup) nut milk
   (we used almond)
70g (½ cup) pumpkin seeds
45g (⅓ cup) cashews
½ tbsp pea or hemp protein
   powder
½ tsp schisandra powder
handful of ice cubes

For the topping (optional)
diced dragon fruit or
   your favourite fruits
sprinkling of RAWnola
   (see page 56)

SERVES 1—2

Place all the ingredients into a high-powered blender and blend on high until the mixture is as smooth as possible.

Pour into a bowl or divide between two bowls and top with dragon fruit or whatever fruits you have available and a sprinkling of RAWnola for added crunch, if you like.

Schisandra
Schisandra has been used in traditional Chinese medicine for over 2,000 years. Known as an adaptogenic berry, it is completely non-toxic and helps to reduce stress. It also helps with overall vitality and is used within Chinese medicine to prolong life, in slowing the ageing process, increasing energy, fighting fatigue, protecting the liver and as a sexual tonic. It is also a significant source of antioxidants and has been shown to possess anti-inflammatory qualities.

Beetroot & Strawberry Overnight Oats

If you've got an early morning start or an important day ahead of you, this is the perfect recipe to prepare in advance to give yourself a head start and make sure you are fuelled up when you need it the most. Beetroot is a great source of a number of vitamins and minerals, and is particularly supportive of the liver's detoxification process (see page 40). Decant this into a sealable jar and devour.

¼ raw beetroot

200g (1 cup) chopped strawberries, plus extra to serve (optional)

125ml (½ cup) almond milk, plus extra to serve

70g (1 cup) gluten-free oats (we use sprouted)

½ tbsp chia seeds

drizzle of honey or coconut syrup, to taste, plus extra to serve

SERVES 1–2

Make sure the beetroot is washed thoroughly. Juice the beetroot and half of the chopped strawberries in a high-powered juicer on high. Pour the juice into a bowl, add the almond milk and oats and stir until the oats are fully submerged in the liquid.

Add the chia seeds to the bowl and stir in to ensure they're covered. Throw in the remaining chopped strawberries and a drizzle of sweetener to taste, stir, then cover with a lid or cling film and place in the fridge overnight.

We like to add another splash of almond milk and a squeeze of honey before eating in the morning, and a few fresh extra chopped strawberries.

45

raw cake

Banana & Peanut Butter Smoothie Bowl

Never trust anyone who doesn't like peanut butter. Banana and PB were born to be together. This is a wonderfully thick and creamy smoothie that will have you wondering how on earth it can be good for you. The baobab and lucuma are optional additions, but they will enhance the nutritional benefits of this smoothie (and your day), while the peanut butter and hemp seeds combine to form a perfect source of protein.

1 ripe banana, plus ½,
  sliced, to decorate
190ml (¾ cup) almond milk
2 tbsp peanut butter (or
  alternative nut butter if
  you don't eat peanuts)
1 tbsp hulled hemp seeds
1 tbsp golden linseed or
  flax seed
½ tbsp baobab powder
  (optional)
½ tbsp lucuma powder
  (optional)
½ tbsp bee pollen (see note on
  safe use on 181), to serve

SERVES 1—2

Place all the ingredients except the banana slices and bee pollen in a high-powered blender and blend on high until creamy and smooth.

Pour into a serving bowl or divide between two serving bowls and decorate with the banana slices and a sprinkling of bee pollen.

47

Power Balls

When energy balls first cropped up we loved trying them, then we noticed that the mass-market products were full of ingredients that were not as appealing as their springy names suggested. So we started to make our own, packing in as many nutrients and superfoods as we could. These days we take it a step further, making balls that are specific to certain needs. We've designed these with three purposes in mind – to help immunity, aid brain function, and encourage radiant skin. If you don't have all of the superfoods, just use whatever you have. The beauty of these balls is that you can freestyle – as long as you taste-test in order to balance the flavours.

Beauty Balls

These bites contain many of the beneficial ingredients that are believed to keep you looking and feeling good and healthy from the inside out. Brazil nuts are a source of selenium, which fights against free radicals thought to cause premature ageing, as do sunflower seeds with their vitamin E; these and camu-camu also help to fight acne and maintain healthy skin. Goji berries provide antioxidants, and collagen helps in the battle against the appearance of ageing. These balls are bouncing with beauty benefits!

48

70g (½ cup) Brazil nuts
35g (¼ cup) sunflower seeds
30g (¼ cup) goji berries
½ tbsp collagen powder
zest of 1 orange
½ tbsp camu-camu powder
2 tbsp maple syrup or
    alternative liquid natural
    sweetener

MAKES 12 BALLS

Place all the ingredients, except the sweetener, in a high-powered food processor and blend on high until fine. Add the syrup and blend again until the mixture sticks together. If it needs help sticking, add a splash of water – no more than 1 tablespoon.

Scoop out 12 equal measures of mixture with a tablespoon and roll it into balls. Place on a plate or baking tray lined with baking paper and leave in the fridge for 1–2 hours. Once set, store in a sealed container in the fridge for up to 1 week.

Above: Beauty balls (green), Immunity balls (red), Brain balls (yellow)

raw breakfasts

Immunity Balls

These have been designed using ingredients that will help build and maintain a healthy immune system. Brazil nuts are rich in selenium, which is essential to enable your white blood cells to fight infection. Cashews and maple syrup are a good source of zinc, which is vital for your body's immune response. Ginger has been found to have anti-microbial properties, and may help in the fight against free radicals. Turmeric is a powerful antioxidant with an active ingredient called curcumin that has been investigated for its anti-viral and anti-fungal properties, as is bee pollen. Lemon is high in vitamin C, adding a little immunity boost.

70g (½ cup) Brazil nuts
70g (½ cup) almonds
30g (¼ cup) cashews
½ tsp freshly grated ginger
¼ tsp turmeric powder
1 tsp bee pollen (see note
    on safe use on p181)
zest of 1 lemon
½ tsp Siberian ginseng
2 tbsp maple syrup
2 tbsp lemon juice

MAKES 12 BALLS

Blend all the ingredients except the maple syrup and lemon juice in a high-powered food processor on high until fine. Add the maple syrup and lemon juice and blend again until the mixture sticks together well.

Using a tablespoon, scoop out 12 equal measures of the mixture and roll into balls with your hands. Place them on a plate or baking tray lined with baking paper and leave in the fridge for 1–2 hours.

Once set, transfer to a sealed container and store in the fridge for up to 1 week.

50

Brain Balls

We designed these to help fight that brain fog – when you're sitting at your desk trying to concentrate yet you find yourself 100 miles away from the task at hand.

Pecans contain copper, which we need to make norepinephrine, a neurotransmitter that your brain cells use to communicate. Research has suggested that antioxidants and other beneficial compounds in walnuts may help to counteract age-related cognitive decline, and even reduce the risk of Alzheimer's. Pumpkin seeds are rich in zinc that is valuable for optimizing memory and thinking power. Hemp seeds are full of good fats that are essential components of a healthy brain. Bee pollen has a high amino acid content that helps to keep the memory functional and the mind alert. Chlorella and spirulina provide vitamins, minerals, omega-3 fatty acids and amino acids, which are essential in supporting brain function. Wheatgrass is found to be high in vitamin K and folates, which support brain cell growth and memory. American ginseng is believed to lower stress levels and help keep the memory sharp.

70g (⅔ cup) pecans

25g (⅓ cup) walnuts

2 tbsp pumpkin seeds

2 tbsp hemp seeds

1 tsp bee pollen (see note on safe use on p181)

1 tsp chia seeds

½ tsp chlorella

½ tsp spirulina

½ tsp wheatgrass

½ tsp American ginseng

2 tbsp coconut syrup or alternative liquid natural sweetener

MAKES 12 BALLS

Place all the ingredients except the sweetener in a high-powered food processor and blend on high until fine and even. Add the sweetener and blend again until the mixture sticks together well. If it needs help sticking together, add a small splash of water – no more than 1 tablespoon.

Using a tablespoon, scoop out 12 equal measures of the mixture and roll it into balls with your hands. Place them on a plate or baking tray lined with baking paper and leave in the fridge for 1–2 hours.

Once set, transfer to a sealed container and store in the fridge for up to 1 week.

Lemon
Tulsi Balls

We love the freshness of the lemon juice in these balls, cutting through the sweet flavours and complementing the spiciness of tulsi. And if you need any more reasons to make these balls, check out the benefits of tulsi, the queen of herbs, on page 186.

65g (½ cup) cashews

70g (½ cup) almonds

35g (½ cup) desiccated coconut

60g (½ cup) pitted Medjool dates

½ tbsp tulsi

zest of 1 lemon

190ml (¾ cup) lemon juice

MAKES 10 BALLS

Place the nuts and desiccated coconut in a high-powered food processor and blend on high just until roughly broken down – you don't want these too fine. Add the dates and blend again quickly to combine, then chuck in the remaining ingredients and blend until the mixture sticks together into a ball.

Using a tablespoon, scoop out 10 equal measures of the mixture and roll it into balls with your hands. Place them on a plate or baking tray lined with baking paper and leave in the fridge for 1–2 hours.

Once set, transfer to a sealed container and store in the fridge for up to 1 week.

52

Flat 42 Swiss Bircher Muesli

This staple was created by our old flatmate, James, at the notorious warehouse Flat 42 in Dalston. We became obsessed with this simple overnight time-saver and we still eat it in the spring and summer months when making porridge just seems like a bit of a faff.

70g (1 cup) gluten-free oats
190ml (¾ cup) almond or
    other nut milk, plus extra
    to loosen (optional)
juice of 1 orange
¼ apple, thinly sliced
40g (¼ cup) raisins
coconut nectar, to your taste
    (or honey if you are not vegan)
zest of 1 lemon
sprinkle of ground cinnamon

SERVES 1

Combine the oats, nut milk and orange juice in a medium bowl, mixing well with a spoon. Cover and leave to soak overnight in the fridge.

The next morning, give the mixture a good stir and add a drop more almond milk if the muesli is too dry.

Spoon into bowls and dress with the apple slices, sprinkle with raisins, squeeze over the coconut nectar and finally sprinkle on the lemon zest and cinnamon. (Too good to be true.)

53

raw cake

Hardihood RAWnola Clusters

For the days when you just can't deny yourself a bowl of cereal for breakfast, do it the grown-up way with raw granola drowned in ice-cold nut milk. We've actually been known to eat this for lunch, dinner, supper and a midnight snack, too.

70g (1 cup) gluten-free oats
(we use sprouted)
90g (½ cup) raw
buckwheat (we use sprouted)
70g (½ cup) almonds
50g (½ cup) pecans
65g (½ cup) cashews
40g (¼ cup) raisins
35g (¼ cup) pumpkin seeds
2 tbsp hemp seeds
3 tbsp coconut flakes
1 tbsp maca powder
¼ tsp ground cinnamon
generous pinch of
Himalayan salt
3 tbsp coconut oil, melted
3 tbsp maple syrup
or coconut syrup

SERVES 4

Preheat the oven to no higher than 42°C or to its lowest temperature.

Blend the oats in a high-powered food processor on high until they become fine, and then add all the remaining ingredients except the coconut oil and syrup. Pulse until the nuts and seeds are broken up but remain chunky.

Place the mixture in a large mixing bowl and pour in the coconut oil and syrup. Mix together by hand, making sure that all of the dry ingredients are covered. Squash together with your fingers, creating some clumps.

Tip out the mixture onto a baking tray lined with baking paper, push the crumbly mixture together and pat it down so that it sticks together as much as possible. Place in the oven for 3 hours, or until the mixture has dried out.

When it has dehydrated, leave it to rest for 10–15 minutes before breaking it up into clusters and storing it in a sealed jar, where it will keep for 1 week.

55

Raw Banana Pancakes

This is a raw, light take on the small American pancake that we all love. When stacked with layers of coconut yoghurt and berries, you will feel like you've had a sumptuous weekend treat. *(Pictured on pages 58-59.)*

2 tbsp flax seed
50g (½ cup) pecans
30g (¼ cup) buckwheat flour
1 banana
125ml (½ cup) almond milk
¼ tsp ground cinnamon
pinch of Himalayan salt
coconut yoghurt and fresh
    berries, to serve

MAKES ABOUT 12 PANCAKES

Preheat the oven to no higher than 42°C or to its lowest temperature.

Grind the flax seed in a high-powered food processor until fine like flour, then transfer it to a bowl and stir in 3 tablespoons of water. Leave for 10–15 minutes to swell and turn into an egg substitute.

Grind the pecans in the clean food processor until they are fine like flour, add in the rest of the ingredients except for the yoghurt and berries and blend until the mixture becomes slightly runny, a little less wet than your usual pancake batter. Place large spoonfuls of the batter onto a plate or baking tray lined with baking paper and smooth into round pancake shapes.

Place in the oven for roughly 1 hour, or until the tops of the pancakes look dried out. Cover the pancakes with another sheet of baking paper and flip the paper over so that the dried tops are now facing down. Leave in the oven to dehydrate for a further 30 minutes–1 hour or until the bases of the pancakes (now flipped to the top) are dry enough for you to peel off the baking paper. If they are dry, take them out of the oven and let them cool on the side before stacking with coconut yoghurt and berries.

Berry & Ginger Chia Seed Jam

We love this recipe. It reminds us of jam-sandwich picnics in the park. It's hugely versatile: if ginger isn't your thing, add a sprinkle of fresh thyme to the mix or swap the fruit for blueberries, blackberries or figs. *(Pictured on page 58.)*

225g (1½ cups) mixed berries
  (we used strawberries
  and raspberries)
1cm piece of fresh ginger,
  peeled and diced
2 tbsp rice malt syrup or
  alternative liquid natural
  sweetener
2 tbsp chia seeds

MAKES 1 JAR

Place the berries and ginger in a high-powered food processor and blend on high to your preferred texture – if you like fine jam, blend it for a little longer, but if you like a few lumps, stop when there are still small chunks remaining. Add the sweetener and chia seeds, stirring by hand until everything is incorporated, adding a little more sweetener, if you like.

Transfer to a clean jar or container, cover with a lid and leave in the fridge to set for no less than 1 hour. This will keep for up to 5 days in the fridge.

57

Chia Seeds
A brilliant source of soluble fibre and omega-3s, chia seeds have a gel-like texture once soaked, making them perfect for helping raw puddings and fruity treats set.

Knockdown Ginger

We love to start the day with a fresh hit of live nutrients. This juice will leave you feeling alert, hydrated and energized. The yellow beetroot has all the benefits of traditional beetroot minus the intense purple colour. If you can't find the yellow variety, regular beetroot will work perfectly.

4 cavolo nero leaves

1 lemon, peeled

2.5cm piece of fresh
   root ginger, peeled

4 handfuls of spinach

½ apple, cored

½ medium-hot chilli

1cm piece of fresh
   turmeric root, peeled

¼ large cucumber

1 yellow raw beetroot

SERVES 1—2

Put all the ingredients in a juicer, juice, pour into a glass or two glasses and enjoy!

Cavolo Nero
Kale's Italian cousin, also known as Tuscan black cabbage, cavolo nero is rich in iron and calcium and at its sweetest and most tender in autumn and winter.

raw breakfasts

Above: Spicy Immunity Shot (top), Adaptogenic Energy Tonic (middle right), Glowing Skin Tonic (bottom)

Glowing
Skin Tonic

If you live in a fast-paced city with its inevitable pollution, do what you can to turn the lights up from the inside. This tried-and-tested complexion brightener fits the bill.

1 pink grapefruit, peeled
125g (1 cup) raspberries
250ml (1 cup) coconut water
2 mint sprigs, leaves picked
½ tsp collagen powder
½ tsp probiotic powder
½ tsp pearl powder (optional)
handful of ice cubes, to serve

SERVES 1–2

Juice the grapefruit in a juicer.

Meanwhile, throw the raspberries and coconut water into a high-powered blender and blend on high until totally smooth. Add the mint leaves, grapefruit juice and powders and blend again until the mint has broken down.

Pour into a glass or divide between two glasses, chuck in the ice and serve.

63

Spicy Immunity Shot

This shot will blow your socks off and support your immune system in one fell swoop. We'll concoct this at the slightest sign of a sniffle. With lemon for alkalizing, turmeric for inflammation, ginger root for stomach settling, apple cider vinegar as a natural antibiotic and mucus remover, echinacea for immunity, astragulus for flu symptoms and chilli for metabolism, there isn't a single ingredient packed in here that doesn't serve a purpose.

1 lemon, peeled
5cm piece of fresh ginger, peeled
1cm piece of fresh turmeric root, peeled
¼ medium-hot chilli, seeds and all
1 rosemary sprig
1 tsp apple cider vinegar
10 drops liquid echinacea (optional)
½ tsp astragalus (optional)

SERVES 1—2

Place the lemon, ginger, turmeric, chilli and rosemary into a juicer and juice.

Add the vinegar to the juice along with the echinacea and astragalus, if using, stirring until combined.

Pour into a glass or divide between two glasses and down it in one.

64

Adaptogenic Energy Tonic

A punchy and flavoursome shot that will keep you feeling energized throughout your day. The addition of the optional adaptogenic superfoods in this recipe will be a huge boost to your energy levels, focus and vibrancy, especially if consumed on a regular basis.

1 carrot

½ raw beetroot

1 lemon, peeled

1cm piece of fresh ginger, peeled

1cm piece of fresh turmeric, peeled

½ tsp American ginseng (optional)

½ tsp Siberian ginseng (optional)

½ tsp astragalus (optional)

SERVES 1—2

Make sure the carrot and beetroot are washed thoroughly, then juice in a high-powered juicer. Add all the remaining ingredients – if they aren't combining well and are lumpy, use a small hand whisk to combine.

Ginseng

American ginseng is an adaptogen – a herb that helps the body adapt to stress. It can have a positive impact on a wide range of health problems, and help maintain overall health and vitality. It is also said to help with memory loss.

Siberian ginseng is known to be an energizer, which helps protect the adrenal glands, increasing their capacity to withstand prolonged stress, which in turn helps fight fatigue and anxiety. It also helps to maintain healthy blood circulation, dispersal of oxygen and other nutrients efficiently around the body and brain.

Immunity Hot Chocolate

For centuries the Incas and Mayans, ancient civilizations of South America, swore by the healing properties of chocolate, and still today their claims cannot be denied. When heated this elixir becomes extra creamy, like a hug in a mug. Be prepared to fall in love with everything and everyone around you.

250ml (1 cup) almond
 or other dairy-free milk
2 tbsp coconut nectar
 or alternative natural
 sweetener
1½ tbsp cacao powder
1 tsp coconut oil
1cm piece of fresh ginger,
 peeled
1cm piece of fresh turmeric
 root, peeled
1 tbsp chaga powder
 (optional)
ground cinnamon,
 for sprinkling

SERVES 2

Place all the ingredients except the cinnamon in a high-powered blender and blend on high until the ginger and turmeric have broken down completely.

Either enjoy cold as a shake or warm up in a saucepan, sprinkle over some cinnamon and enjoy a heart-opening, immunity-boosting, night-on-the-sofa elixir.

66

Nut Another Smoothie Bowl

We start the day with this chilled-out alternative to porridge when we want warming spices and comforting banana without the heat.

65-70g (½ cup) mixed
  nuts, such as Brazil,
  almond, cashews
20g (¼ cup) gluten-free oats
  (we use sprouted)
125ml (½ cup) almond
  or other nut milk
1½ bananas, frozen
¼ tsp ground cinnamon
1 tsp coconut sugar
1 tsp lucuma
½ tsp probiotic powder
pinch of Himalayan salt
190ml (¾ cup) filtered water

For the topping (optional)
chopped strawberries
ground cinnamon
your favourite seeds,
  (we love pumpkin, hemp
  and golden linseed)

SERVES 1—2

Blend all the ingredients together in a high-powered blender on high, adding the water last, a little at a time, until the smoothie is your preferred consistency.

Pour into a bowl and serve scattered with your preferred toppings, if you like.

Probiotic Powder
Probiotics are live bacteria and yeasts that benefit our gut health. Known as 'good bacteria', they help to balance our digestive system, process some forms of fibre and may help to keep our bowel function regular. The different strains of bacteria have varying effects; they can produce a number of vitamins, including B6 and B12, aid in the absorption of various minerals and can help to treat diarrhoea.

Matcha Mint Iced Cooler

A refreshing, energizing, achingly cool cooler, we love to enjoy this in the garden at our studio. It's the perfect summertime hydrating drink with the uplifting benefits of matcha thrown in.

juice of 1 orange
6–8 fresh mint leaves
½ tbsp matcha powder
juice of ½ lemon
750ml (3 cups) sparkling
   water
ice cubes, to serve

SERVES 2—4

Pour the orange juice into a high-powered blender and add the mint leaves and matcha powder. Blend until the leaves start to break down, then pour into a medium jug, adding the lemon juice and sparkling water.

Pour over ice to serve.

68

Matcha
A powdered green tea – far more potent than regular green tea – matcha contains high quantities of polyphenol compounds (catechins), antioxidants that are said to have anti-carcinogenic properties. Its bitter flavour can be overwhelming, so use it sparingly.

raw breakfasts

raw cake

Anti-inflammatory Golden Milk

We've come to learn that inflammation in one form or another is at the root of many bodily ailments. Turmeric is one of nature's powerful anti-inflammatory wonders and should help to counteract this, keeping you feeling light, clear-headed and energized, while the addition of black pepper helps the blood to better absorb the curcumin from the turmeric.

145g (1 cup) almonds,
    soaked overnight
140g (1 cup) pumpkin seeds,
    soaked overnight
500ml (2 cups) filtered water
30g (¼ cup) pitted soft dates
2.5cm piece of fresh
    turmeric root, peeled, or
    use 3 tbsp ground if you
    can't get fresh
½ tsp vanilla powder
pinch of black pepper

SERVES 2–4

Drain the almonds and pumpkin seeds, rinse under cold running water, drain again and place in a high-powered blender along with all the other ingredients and blend on high until as smooth as possible.

Pour through a nut milk bag into a large bowl or measuring jug. Squeeze the bag to make sure that all the liquid comes through and discard the pulp left in the bag.

71

Pour the milk into a clean bottle or jar and refrigerate until ready to serve. This will keep for 2–3 days in the fridge.

Shroom Shake

Sorry to disappoint, this ain't that kind of mushroom shake. No full moon parties here...

Medicinal mushrooms have been on our radar for a few years now, but it is only recently that we've noticed them creeping their way onto more shop shelves. Powerful adaptogens (see page 180), they should be used sparingly but often for optimal results. This shake is smooth and delicious, with a whole host of benefits.

250ml (1 cup) homemade
   nut milk (see pages 21–25)
½ tsp chaga powder
½ tsp reishi
½ tsp cordyceps
½ tsp ground cinnamon
1 tsp coconut oil
1 tsp coconut sugar,
   to taste (optional)

SERVES 2

Add all the ingredients to a small saucepan and heat gently, whisking until all are well combined and the shake is nicely warmed. Pour into a mug or glass and enjoy.

TIP: Don't worry if you only have one variety of these mushrooms – just adjust the amount of the one you are using. Feel free to include any Chinese medicinal mushrooms for a powerful healing shake.

72

Brown Rice Horchata

We'd been lusting after horchata from afar for some time, and it wasn't until we got to LA that we first tasted the Mexican real deal. This recipe originates from a plant-based alternative that blew our minds; the addition of lucuma gives it that extra spark and the cinnamon stick really adds depth of flavour.

225g (1 cup) brown rice
1 litre (4 cups) filtered water
1 cinnamon stick
85g (¼ cup) maple syrup
250ml (1 cup) almond or
    other non-dairy milk
1 tbsp lucuma (optional)
½ tsp vanilla powder
½ tsp ground cinnamon
ice cubes, to serve

SERVES 2—4

Put the rice in a bowl or jug with the water and cinnamon stick, cover with a cloth or tea towel and leave to soak at room temperature overnight.

The next day, remove the cinnamon stick and blend the rice with the water in a high-powered blender. Pour through a nut milk bag into a bowl, squeezing out all of the milk. Return the milk to a clean blender with all the other ingredients, except the ice, and pulse to combine.

Serve over ice. This will keep in the fridge for 3 days.

73

Most days we are constantly on the go, and sometimes we just need a hit of something lovely to help us along. We love making these fun indulgent treats. They can be eaten at your leisure, whether you're on the go or making repeated visits to the fridge. Get your mates involved in whipping up a batch, or make them with the children, but take it easy on the bowl-licking when you're using cacao – that stuff's dynamite: there has been many an occasion where we have been found giggling and bouncing off the ceilings after getting high from too much quality control!

The Modern Scone

This is a modern, raw take on a traditional English favourite. Our mums, Ingrid and Rachel, love them, so they come with the mothers' seal of approval. These are a must for any revitalized afternoon tea menu. *(Pictured on pages 74-75.)*

For the scones
160g (2 cups) cashews
210g (3 cups) gluten-free oats
1 tbsp lucuma (optional)
40g (¼ cup) raisins
65g (½ cup) coconut sugar
generous pinch of
    Himalayan salt
62-125ml (¼-½ cup) nut milk
    (we used almond)
juice and zest of 1 lemon
Berry & Chia Seed Jam,
    to serve (page 57)

For the coconut cream
200g (1 cup) coconut butter
2 tbsp coconut syrup

MAKES 7—8 SCONES

Preheat the oven to no higher than 42°C or to its lowest temperature.

Place the cashews and oats in a high-powered food processor and blend on high to make a fine flour. Pour into a large mixing bowl and stir in the lucuma, raisins, coconut sugar and salt. Clean out the bowl of the food processor.

Pour in the nut milk to the mixture, a little at a time, then the lemon juice and zest and knead the dough with your hands until well combined. Separate into roughly 7 or 8 small balls, and place on a baking sheet. Dehydrate in the oven for 3–4 hours or until the outside is dry. Remove from the oven and leave to rest for 10 minutes.

For the cream, add the coconut butter and coconut syrup to the clean food processor and blend until smooth.

Split the scones and serve with the coconut cream and some Berry & Chia Seed Jam.

77

Banana Dough Bites

Smooth, creamy maca takes these outrageously good dough bites to the next level. Keep in the fridge or store in a recycled jam jar for rich pickings on the move.

For the dough
195g (1½ cups) cashews
15g (¼ cup) gluten-free oats
100g (¾ cup) coconut sugar
large pinch of salt
¼ medium banana
3 tbsp maca powder
½ tsp vanilla powder
3 tbsp rice malt syrup
1 tbsp melted coconut oil

For the chocolate mix
50g (¼ cup) coconut oil, melted
60g (¾ cup) cacao powder
100g (½ cup) cacao butter, melted
85g (¼ cup) rice malt syrup

First make the chocolate mix. Combine all the ingredients for the chocolate in a high-powered food processor on high. If the mixture isn't runny enough, add a little more coconut oil until you get the perfect dipping consistency. Pour a small puddle of the chocolate mix (around 3 tablespoons) onto a sheet of baking paper and transfer to the freezer for about 10 minutes to set. Leave the rest of the chocolate mix to one side, and clean out the bowl of the food processor.

Next, start the dough. Blitz the nuts and oats in the clean food processor until fine, then add all other ingredients and blend until the mixture forms a doughy texture. Transfer to a large bowl.

Remove the chocolate from the freezer once it has set and crumble it into pieces. Drop these chips into the dough quickly – they may get a little melty, but that's fine. Place the dough in the freezer for 10 minutes as a whole block to cool off, then take it out and roll it into medium balls and place the balls on a sheet of baking paper.

Dip and roll your balls in the dipping chocolate and place them back on the baking paper using a spoon or fork. Place in the fridge to set for 1 hour – then devour. We challenge you to eat only one!

78

Cashews
Coconut sugar
Vanilla beans

maca
Gluten free oats
cacao
cacao nibs

raw treats

Raw Hot
Cross Buns

We're not religious, but we'll worship at the church of these buns any day. It's always fun to recreate the classics without using traditional techniques and these were a real breakthrough. Oozing with exactly the same crunch and flavours as the traditional hot cross bun that you know and love, these nutritionally balanced buns are bunderful.

For the buns

145g (1 cup) almonds

70g (1 cup) gluten-free oats

125g (1 cup) pitted dates,
    soaked for 5 minutes to soften

½ tsp vanilla powder

½ tsp ground cinnamon

½ tsp ground ginger

2 tbsp maca powder

zest of 1 orange

3 generous pinches
    of Himalayan salt

120g (¾ cup) raisins

For the cashew cream cross

195g (1½ cups) cashews,
    soaked for 1–2 hours
    and drained

juice of 1 lemon

½ tsp vanilla powder

3 tbsp rice malt syrup
    or alternative natural
    liquid sweetener

MAKES 6 BUNS

Preheat the oven to no higher than 42°C or to its lowest temperature.

First make the cashew cream. Blend all the ingredients in a high-powered blender – we used a Vitamix to get this ultra-smooth. Transfer the cream to a piping bag and put in the fridge to set for 2–3 hours.

Meanwhile, make the buns. Blend all the ingredients, except the raisins, with 3 tablespoons of water in a high-powered food processor for 2–3 minutes until it becomes a dough-like consistency, then remove the dough from the bowl of the processor and knead in the raisins. Shape the dough into six balls and place on a baking sheet, spaced slightly apart, squashing them down slightly. Cut a cross shape into the top of each bun.

Put the buns in the oven for 1½–2 hours to dehydrate. Remove from the oven and leave to cool.

Once cool, pipe the cashew cream into the cross indentations on top of the buns and eat!

80

raw treats

Cacao Chaga Doughnuts

We love this recipe because it's an all-round crowd pleaser. Inspired by the chocolate doughnuts of your dreams, the uplifting effects of cacao and the added benefits of chaga make for one powerfully packed, sumptuous, doughnut experience. Dunk in chocolate or leave them baring all, the choice is yours. (*Pictured on pages 84–85.*)

105g (1½ cups) gluten-free oats

40g (½ cup) walnuts

70g (½ cup) almonds

35g (¼ cup) sunflower seeds

2 tbsp chia seeds

1 tbsp chaga powder

4 tbsp cacao powder

45g (⅓ cup) coconut sugar

½ tsp ground cinnamon

½ tsp vanilla powder

2 large pinches of salt

85ml (½ cup) coconut oil, melted

115g (⅓ cup) rice malt syrup

To decorate (optional)

Raw Chocolate
    (see page 26), for dipping
fresh petals, crushed nuts
    or desiccated coconut

MAKES 18 MINI DOUGHNUTS
OR YOU CAN MIX SMALL AND LARGE SIZES

Preheat the oven to no higher than 42°C or to its lowest temperature.

Place the oats, nuts and seeds in a high-powered food processor and blend on high until as smooth as possible. Add the rest of the ingredients, adding the coconut oil and rice malt syrup last. Once the mixture is blended, make sure it is sticky enough and doesn't crumble apart – if it does, add another squirt of syrup.

Press the mixture into the doughnut moulds of your choice – we used a mixture of small and large moulds. Place in the oven for 2–3 hours, or until they have dried out slightly. Remove from the oven and leave to cool on a wire rack, if needed, for 10–15 minutes.

Drizzle or dunk the doughnuts, if you like, into raw chocolate, sprinkle with petals, nuts or desiccated coconut (see pages 178–179 for topping inspiration) and place in the fridge until the chocolate hardens. They will keep for up to 5 days, undecorated, in the fridge.

Matcha Pistachio Doughnuts

These matcha doughnuts became instant legends among our studio mates, who regularly get to sample our creations. On the more savoury side of sweet, these are great any time of day and pack an added punch in the form of the deliciously mellow matcha. Matcha + doughnuts equals a winning combo. (*Pictured on pages 84–85.*)

130g (1 cup) cashews
105g (1½ cups) gluten-free oats
40g (½ cup) desiccated coconut
2 tbsp matcha powder
generous pinch of
    Himalayan salt
generous 125ml (½ cup)
    rice malt syrup
25g (¼ cup) pistachios,
    plus extra, finely chopped,
    for decoration
Raw Chocolate (see page 26),
    for dipping, or coconut cream
    (see page 77) (optional)

**MAKES 18 MINI DOUGHNUTS
OR YOU CAN MIX SMALL AND LARGE SIZES**

Preheat the oven to no higher than 42°C or to its lowest temperature.

Place the nuts, oats and desiccated coconut in a high-powered food processor and blend on high until fine. Throw in all the remaining ingredients except the pistachios and chocolate and blend until well combined and sticky.

Place the finely chopped pistachio pieces in the bottom of the doughnut moulds (we used some big rings and some small), then press the dough into the moulds on top of the pistachios and place in the oven for 3–4 hours, or until the doughnuts have dried out slightly. Remove from the oven, remove from the moulds and place on a wire rack to cool completely.

If you like, you can decorate some of the doughnuts by dipping the tops in Raw Chocolate or piping on some coconut cream and sprinkling with the extra pistachios. They will keep for up to 5 days, undecorated, in the fridge.

83

raw cake

Beetroot Red Velvet Cupcakes

This recipe brings everyone's favourite cupcake bang up to date. We were both raised in the noughties, and this is one of our favourite raw throwbacks. Wear double denim while eating.

For the cupcakes

145g (1 cup) almonds

65g (½ cup) cashews

300g (2 cups) washed and grated raw beetroot

60g (½ cup) pitted Medjool dates

100g (¾ cup) coconut sugar

½ tsp vanilla powder

For the coconut frosting

115g (1½ cups) desiccated coconut

60ml (¼ cup) filtered water

85g (¼ cup) rice malt syrup

50g (¼ cup) coconut oil, melted

MAKES 8–10 CUPCAKES

Place the almonds and cashews in a high-powered food processor and blend on high until they become fine like flour. Add the remaining ingredients to the food processor and blend until smooth.

Spoon the mixture into 8–10 paper cases set on a baking tray and transfer to the freezer for 30 minutes until set.

Meanwhile, make the frosting. Soak the desiccated coconut in the filtered water for 1 hour or more, then add all the ingredients to a high-powered blender. Blend until absolutely smooth and then blend some more – this will be what turns the frosting light and fluffy!

Using a thick piping bag, swirl the coconut frosting onto the beetroot cupcakes and leave in the fridge for 1–2 hours to set. They will keep in the fridge for up to 5 days.

Raspberry Peanut Butter Cups

Our dads first introduced us to the delights of peanut butter and jam on toast, so we suppose it's fair to say that these raspberry peanut butter cups are Dad-inspired. Downright delicious, these definitely keep the PBJ dream alive.

For the chocolate mix
250ml (1 cup) cacao oil, melted

60g (¾ cup) cacao powder

255g (¾ cup) rice malt syrup or alternative liquid natural sweetener

50g (¼ cup) cacao butter, melted

For the peanut butter filling
130g (½ cup) peanut butter (no added sugar natural variety)

30g (¼ cup) coconut sugar

85g (¼ cup) rice malt syrup or alternative liquid natural sweetener

50g (¼ cup) coconut oil, melted

raspberries, whole or chopped in half, to decorate

MAKES 20–25 CUPS

Place all the chocolate mix ingredients in a high-powered food processor and blend on high until well combined (try not to over-mix). Transfer to a squeezy bottle, or a bowl if you don't have one.

Place all of the filling ingredients in a medium bowl and stir to combine until smooth.

To assemble, take 20–25 small cupcake moulds or paper cases and line them up on a chopping board or tray that will fit into your fridge. Divide roughly half the mixture equally between the cases. Place the cases in the fridge for 15–20 minutes until set.

Spoon a dollop of the peanut butter filling into each of the cases, on top of the set chocolate mix, smoothing it out with a spoon. Press in half a raspberry flat on top, or you can place a whole raspberry upright so that it sticks out from the chocolate.

Pour the remaining chocolate mix into each cup, covering the raspberry and peanut butter filling. The upright raspberries will poke through the chocolate nicely. Place back into the fridge for a further 20–30 minutes before serving. Having only one will be your problem…

88

raw treats

Banana Loaf & Cream Frosting

We were both born and raised on banana bread, so it only made sense to recreate our childhood favourite. This is just as heart-warming as the one Grandma used to make, only raw and enhanced with the benefits of natural nutrients. Dollop on the deliciously creamy frosting generously.

For the loaf
coconut oil, for greasing
100g (1 cup) pecans
80g (1 cup) whole walnuts, plus 40g (½ cup), roughly chopped and extra to serve (optional)
70g (1 cup) gluten-free oats
125g (1 cup) pitted dates, roughly chopped
4 small ripe bananas
30g (¼ cup) coconut sugar
1 tbsp ground ginger
2 tbsp rice malt syrup or alternative natural liquid sweetener
pinch of salt

For the cream frosting
1 small banana
1 x 400ml can coconut milk (place in the fridge overnight, only use the top layer of cream)
2 tbsp rice malt syrup

SERVES 8–10

Preheat the oven to no higher than 42°C or to its lowest temperature. Line a 450g loaf tin with baking paper and rub the sides with coconut oil.

Place the pecans and the 80g (1 cup) whole walnuts and oats in a high-powered food processor and blend on high until they form a flour-like consistency. Transfer to a large mixing bowl, add the chopped walnuts and the dates to the dry mixture and set aside.

Add the bananas to the food processor and blend on high until smooth, then tip in the coconut sugar, ginger, sweetener and salt and blend again. Stir the banana mix into the dry ingredients until completely combined. Press into the tin and dehydrate in the oven for 3 hours. Clean out the bowl of the food processor.

Meanwhile, make the cream frosting. Blend the banana in the clean food processor. Scoop out the layer of cream on the top of the watery coconut milk, then add the cream and syrup to the banana and blend again for a few seconds. Transfer to a bowl and place in the fridge for 2–3 hours until it stiffens.

To assemble, take the loaf out of the tin and let it rest for 30 minutes at room temperature, then top with the banana cream, and some extra chopped walnuts, if you wish. Slice away!

raw treats

raw cake

Raspberry Cream Cacao Stacks

Like an Oreo, only more chic and raw. We love to make these stacked cookies when raspberries are in season. They're so irresistibly flavoursome when coupled with the chocolate. They are the perfect side-kick to your afternoon cup of green tea.

For the cookies
145g (1 cup) almonds
50g (½ cup) pecans
125g (1 cup) pitted soft dates
1 tsp vanilla powder
2 tbsp coconut sugar
20g (¼ cup) cacao powder
2 pinches of salt

For the raspberry cream
125g (1 cup) raspberries
3 tbsp coconut butter
2 tbsp rice malt syrup

MAKES 8–10 STACKS

First make the cookies. Place the nuts in a high-powered food processor and blend on high until fine, then add all the remaining ingredients and blend on high until well mixed. If the mixture isn't sticking together well because your dates aren't very soft, add a tiny splash of water. Clean out the bowl of the food processor and roll out the mixture onto a piece of baking paper using a rolling pin, or press down flat between two sheets with a book.

Using a 5cm or 6cm cookie cutter, cut out 16–20 cookies, re-rolling the dough as necessary, and place the cookies on a tray in the fridge for 1–2 hours until set.

Meanwhile, make the raspberry cream. Blend all the ingredients together in the clean food processor until smooth. Transfer to a bowl and place in the fridge for 1 hour or until the cream has hardened slightly.

To assemble the stacks, take one cookie, dollop a large tablespoon of raspberry cream onto one side and place another cookie on top. Place in the fridge for a further 30 minutes to help the cream set slightly. Enjoy straight from the fridge!

93

raw cake

Salted Caramel Crunch Bars

We've yet to meet anyone who can resist the temptation of these triple-layered bars, so keep them under lock and key! With biscuit, caramel and chocolate, they're everyone's favourites rolled into one.

For the biscuit base
145g (1 cup) almonds
44g (¼ cup) raw buckwheat
125g (1 cup) pitted dates,
  soaked for 2 minutes,
  or use soft Medjool dates
20g (¼ cup) desiccated
  coconut
1 tbsp tahini paste
3 generous pinches
  of Himalayan salt

For the salted caramel layer
250g (2 cups) pitted dates,
  soaked
2 tbsp tahini paste
3 tbsp coconut oil, melted
2 tbsp rice malt syrup
  or alternative liquid
  natural sweetener
3-5 pinches of salt,
  according to taste

For the crunch layer
70g (½ cup) almonds
35g (¼ cup) pumpkin seeds
25g (¼ cup) cacao nibs
2 tbsp raw buckwheat

For the chocolate drizzle topping
Raw Chocolate (see page 26)

MAKES 8—10 BARS

Line a 20cm square baking tin with baking paper.

First make the biscuit base. Place the almonds and buckwheat in a high-powered food processor and blend until chopped but not too fine. Then add all the remaining ingredients and blend until well combined. Press into the base of the baking tin and clean out the bowl of the food processor.

For the salted caramel, drain then blend the dates in the clean food processor on high before adding the tahini and coconut oil. Blend again, making sure you get this as smooth as possible. Stop a few times and scrape down the sides with a spatula. Add salt to taste – we love to make this layer nice and salty. Smooth this over the biscuit base in the tin and place in the fridge while you prepare the next layer.

For the crunch layer, roughly chop the almonds and pumpkin seeds using a sharp knife. We don't use a blender so that we can keep this nice and chunky. Combine the almonds and pumpkin seeds with the cacao nibs and buckwheat in a large bowl. Press this dry mix into the salted caramel layer. Finish with a layer of Raw Chocolate – drizzle it over the top of the nuts from side to side.

Transfer to the fridge for 1 hour to set, before cutting into 8-10 bars. They will keep well in the fridge for up to 1 week.

95

Rocky Road

This is one of our oldest recipes. When we first made them we couldn't believe how good they were and how quick they were to create. It might be fair to say that they gave us faith that there was a whole world of raw desserts out there just waiting to be discovered. These bites are simultaneously soft, crunchy and seriously moreish.

For the dry mix
155g (1 cup) dried apricots
   (sulphur free)
40g (½ cup) walnuts
60g (½ cup) hazelnuts
80g (½ cup) mixed currants
   or raisins
55g (½ cup) goji berries

For the chocolate mix
150g (¾ cup) coconut oil,
   melted
60g (¾ cup) cacao powder
30g (¼ cup) coconut sugar
170g (½ cup) rice malt syrup
60g (½ cup) pitted dates,
   soaked for 30 minutes

MAKES 9–12 PIECES

Line a 15cm square baking tin with baking paper.

Place all the dry mix ingredients in a high-powered food processor and pulse on high until just broken up and mixed together but still chunky. Transfer to a large mixing bowl and clean out the bowl of the food processor.

Next, make the chocolate mix. Add the coconut oil, cacao, coconut sugar and syrup to the clean food processor and blend on high, then add the dates and blend until smooth and combined. Make sure you don't over-mix the chocolate or it can separate. If this happens and there is a lot of extra oil, add in some more cacao powder and malt syrup until it becomes smooth.

Pour the chocolate mix over the dry mix and stir together with a large spoon until well combined. Scoop into the baking tin, pressing the mixture down to ensure it is compact. Place in the fridge for 3–4 hours or the freezer for 1 hour until it has completely set, then cut into 9–12 pieces. They will keep well in the fridge for up to 7 days.

96

raw treats

Oatmeal & Raisin Cookies

Sometimes there's really no point in reinventing the wheel. We've loved this simple, squidgy classic forever and this no-frills raw version is every bit as robust as the original. An absolute favourite of ours – dunk these cookies into tea or almond milk for best results!

70g (1 cup) rolled oats
60g (½ cup) pitted dates
65g (½ cup) coconut sugar
80g (½ cup) raisins, plus
   extra for decorating
1 tsp ground cinnamon
½ tsp vanilla powder
4 tbsp rice malt syrup
   or alternative liquid
   natural sweetener
1 tbsp melted coconut oil

MAKES 8 COOKIES

Preheat the oven to no higher than 42°C or to its lowest temperature, and line a baking sheet with baking paper.

Place the oats and dates in a high-powered food blender and blend on high until fine. Add all the remaining ingredients and blend briefly, just until everything is well combined – you don't want the raisins to become too fine.

Separate the mixture into 8 even-sized balls, using your hands, and press down into flattened cookie shapes on the baking paper.

Place the cookies in the oven for 3–4 hours to dehydrate, then decorate with extra raisins. They will keep well in the fridge for up to 1 week.

98

raw treats

Fate
Cookies

Fig + date = fate. Perfect partners in crime, these two have conspired to keep you going back to the cookie jar. You can't escape your fate.

145g (1 cup) dried figs

60g (½ cup) pitted dates

50g (½ cup) pecans

70g (½ cup) almonds

½ tbsp vanilla powder

2 tbsp rice malt syrup
  or alternative liquid
  natural sweetener

2 tbsp maca powder (optional)

3 tbsp melted coconut oil

2 tbsp sunflower seeds
  (optional)

pinch of salt

MAKES 10—12 COOKIES

Preheat the oven to no higher than 42°C or to its lowest temperature, and line a baking sheet with baking paper.

Place the figs, dates and nuts in a high-powered food processor and blend on high until mixed and quite fine. Add all the remaining ingredients and blend again until well combined.

Separate the mixture into 10–12 even-sized balls, using your hands, and press each ball down into flattened cookie shapes on the baking paper.

Place the cookies in the oven for 3–4 hours to dehydrate. They will keep well in the fridge for up to 1 week.

Dark Chocolate Truffles

50g (¼ cup) coconut oil, melted
40g (½ cup) cacao powder,
　plus extra to coat
125g (½ cup) rice malt syrup
3 tbsp cacao butter, melted
3 tbsp coconut cream
finely chopped hazelnuts or
　cacao powder, to decorate

Luxuriously rich, these are next-level gooey and melt in your mouth like their traditional counterparts. Make a batch and box them up – they make great gifts for every occasion.

MAKES 10–12 TRUFFLES

Place all the ingredients except for the hazelnuts and cacao powder in a high-powered food processor and blend on high, then dollop the mixture into a bowl, cover and leave to set in the fridge for 2–3 hours – make sure it doesn't set completely hard, though, as it needs to be soft enough to scoop.

Scoop the chocolate into 10–12 balls with a teaspoon (we roll them in glove-covered palms for ease).

Roll the balls in cacao powder or finely chopped hazelnuts, then chill in the fridge until needed. They will keep well in the fridge for up to 1 week.

101

Jon Snow Balls

65g (½ cup) cashews

35g (½ cup) desiccated coconut,
   plus extra for rolling

2 tbsp rice malt syrup

½ tsp vanilla powder

generous pinch of salt

coconut oil, for greasing

These luminous, dusted delights are a subtle nod to everyone's favourite *Game of Thrones* hero. Winter is coming.

MAKES 16 BALLS

Place the cashews and coconut in a high-powered food processor and blend on high until as fine as possible. Add the remaining ingredients to the processor, adding a dash of water if the mixture isn't sticky enough to roll.

Roll the mixture into 16 balls using the palms of your hands and then coat your palms with coconut oil before rolling each ball in desiccated coconut. Transfer to a tray and chill in the fridge to set. They will keep in the fridge for 1 week.

102

raw treats

Ginger & Apricot Bars

These bars are great. You can fix them up on a Sunday and keep going back for more throughout the week. We love the mellow taste of dried apricots offset by the spiciness of the fresh ginger.

75g (½ cup) dried apricots
  (sulphur free)
35g (½ cup) desiccated coconut
65g (½ cup) cashews
65g (½ cup) macadamias
3 tbsp rice malt syrup
  or alternative liquid
  natural sweetener
3 tbsp grated fresh root ginger,
  plus extra (optional)
dried coconut flakes, to decorate

MAKES 6–8 BARS

Line a 15cm square baking tin with baking paper.

Place all the ingredients except for the coconut flakes in a high-powered food processor and blend on high until as smooth as possible. Taste, then add more ginger if you like.

Transfer the mixture to the baking tin and press down the mixture evenly. Press some coconut flakes on top of the mixture and transfer to the freezer for 1 hour to set.

Once set, cut into 6–8 bars and enjoy. The bars will keep in the fridge for up to 5 days.

Cold Brew Chocolate Cake

Who doesn't go weak at the knees at the thought of chocolate and coffee together? This gorgeously glutinous nutritional melting pot is our take on a rich, raw sponge cake.

For the cake
500g (4 cups) pitted dates
520g (4 cups) cashews
5 tbsp concentrated
    cold-brew coffee
    (see page 183)
40g (½ cup) cacao powder
65g (⅓ cup) coconut oil, melted
1 tsp vanilla powder
1 tsp salt
chopped cashews or
    cacao nibs, to decorate

For the coffee frosting
260g (2 cups) cashews,
    soaked for 2 hours
    and drained
250ml (1 cup) concentrated
    cold-brew coffee
170g (½ cup) rice malt syrup
    or maple syrup
100g (½ cup) coconut oil, melted
1 x 400ml can full-fat coconut
    milk (place in the fridge
    overnight, only use the top
    layer of cream)

TIP: if the coffee flavour needs a boost, whizz 1 tbsp beans or organic coffee granules in a blender and add to the mix

SERVES 6—8

Line a 15cm square baking tin with baking paper.

To make the cake, place the dates in a high-powered food processor and blend on high until they become a paste – you may need to stop the machine and scrape down the sides a few times until the mixture is nice and smooth. Set aside in a bowl and clean out the bowl of the food processor.

Place the cashews in the clean food processor and blend until fine, add the coffee and cacao and blend until as smooth as possible. Incorporate the remaining ingredients plus the date paste and blend until nicely combined. If there is too much oil, add some more cacao powder. Press half the mixture into the baking tin and place in the fridge to set. Clean out the bowl of the food processor.

To make the frosting, blend the cashews with the coffee in the clean food processor on high until smooth. Add the remaining ingredients, adding the coconut cream last. Transfer to a bowl and place in the fridge for 2–3 hours until it stiffens up.

Spread half the frosting mix on top of your first cake layer, transfer to the fridge for 30 minutes until set or very firm. Press the rest of your cake mix over the frosting, transfer to the fridge for 30 minutes again until set or very firm.

Remove the cake from the tin once set and smooth over the remaining frosting. Transfer to the fridge for 1–2 hours until the cream is firm enough for you to cut the cake (ideally leave overnight, if you can wait!). Sprinkle with chopped nuts or cacao nibs to decorate.

105

raw treats

Hazelnut & Chocolate Cupcakes

This has to be one of our absolute favourite recipes and even though our cupcake days are firmly behind us, there's still something to be said for a cake that's equal parts cake to frosting.

For the base

125g (1 cup) hazelnuts,
   plus extra, finely chopped,
   to decorate
145g (1 cup) almonds
90g (½ cup) raw buckwheat
125g (1 cup) pitted dates
65g (½ cup) coconut sugar
40g (½ cup) cacao powder
4 tbsp cacao nibs
1 tsp grated nutmeg
generous pinch of
   Himalayan salt
4–5 tbsp water

For the hazelnut cream

190g (1½ cups) hazelnuts,
   soaked for 3 hours and drained
180ml (¾ cup) coconut cream
   (use the boxed version or leave
   a tin in the fridge overnight, then
   scoop off the cream on top)
20g (¼ cup) cacao powder
170g (½ cup) rice malt syrup
   or alternative liquid
   natural sweetener
100g (½ cup) coconut oil,
   melted
60g (½ cup) pitted dates,
   soaked until soft
1 tsp vanilla powder
60ml (¼ cup) almond milk

Preheat the oven to no higher than 42°C or to its lowest temperature.

First make the base. Place all the nuts, the buckwheat and dates in a high-powered food processor and blend on high until fine, then add all the remaining ingredients except the water and blend again. Add the water, 1 tablespoon at a time, until the mixture sticks together well but isn't too sticky and wet.

Press the base mixture into 10 muffin or cupcake moulds. Ensure the base of each is covered, but leave enough space in the centres to pipe in the cream topping. Place the muffin or cupcake moulds on a baking tray and dehydrate in the oven for 2 hours or until they have dried out nicely. Clean out the bowl of the food processor.

For the cream, blend the soaked hazelnuts in the clean food processor until they are smooth. Add the remaining ingredients and blend until the mixture is creamy – this should take 5–10 minutes depending on your machine. The cream should be a soft, stiff texture, not too runny or hard. If it's too runny, add some more cacao, and if too hard a splash of almond milk should do the trick. If your food processor doesn't get the mixture smooth enough, transfer it to a high-speed blender like a Vitamix to get the perfect lump-free consistency. Pour the cream into a piping bag fitted with a wide nozzle.

Pipe the cream into each base, sprinkle with a few finely chopped hazelnuts and leave to set in the fridge overnight. Pop the cupcakes out of the moulds carefully once the cream has set. They will keep in the fridge for 5 days.

107

Nut-free Double Chocolate Brownies

A nut-free version of one of our first ever recipes, these chocolate brownies are every bit as indulgent as their nutty friend. In fact, we actually find the cacao to be more potent in this recipe than any of our others. Add in the benefits of the chia seeds and you've got yourself a powerhouse of energy and yumminess. Ideal for friends with nut allergies or anyone who fancies a change from nuts.

For the brownies

70g (½ cup) pumpkin seeds

70g (½ cup) sunflower seeds

35g (¼ cup) chia seeds

65g (½ cup) coconut sugar

25g (¼ cup) cacao nibs

1 tbsp maca powder

1 tbsp rice malt syrup

190g (1½ cups) pitted dates, soaked

40g (½ cup) cacao powder

For the frosting

60g (½ cup) pitted dates, soaked

20g (¼ cup) cacao powder

30g (¼ cup) coconut sugar

85g (¼ cup) rice malt syrup or maple syrup

2 tbsp coconut oil, melted

MAKES 10—12 BROWNIES

Line a 15cm square baking tin with baking paper.

Blend all the brownie ingredients except the dates and cacao powder in a high-powered food processor on high for 2–3 minutes until they are as fine as possible. Add the dates and cacao powder and blend until the mixture is nice and gooey and totally combined. Press into the baking tin and clean out the bowl of the food processor.

For the frosting, blend the dates in the clean food processor on high until nice and smooth. Add the remaining ingredients and blend until the mixture is gooey and creamy.

Spread the frosting on top of the brownie mixture, creating texture in the top with your spoon. Set in the fridge until the frosting is firm, for about 3 hours or ideally overnight. Cut into 10–12 squares. They will keep well in the fridge for up to 1 week.

Raw Fig Rolls

An Egyptian classic made here on the streets of Shoreditch. Who'd have guessed it? These fig rolls are absolute party starters. Do the big reveal during an afternoon catch-up with friends.

For the dough
95g (¾ cup) pitted dates
35g (½ cup) gluten-free oats
35g (½ cup) desiccated coconut
½ tsp ground cinnamon
60ml (¼ cup) orange juice
pinch of salt

For the fig paste
145g (1 cup) dried figs,
   soaked for 1 hour
60g (½ cup) pitted dates
zest of 1 orange

MAKES 6–8 ROLLS

Preheat the oven to no higher than 42°C or to its lowest temperature.

First make the dough. Blend the dates, oats and coconut in a high-powered food processor on high until fine, then add the remaining ingredients and blend until the mixture is soft and combined. Roll out the mixture evenly onto a piece of baking paper on a baking tray and place in the oven for 2 hours or until the top is dried out. Clean out the bowl of the food processor.

Meanwhile, make the fig paste. Remove the stalks from the soaked figs, add to the clean food processor with the dates and orange zest. Mix until combined and gooey – you might have to stop the mixer a couple of times and scrape down the sides. Set to one side in a bowl until the dough is ready.

Remove the dough from the oven and place a sheet of baking paper and a cold baking sheet over the top. Flip the dough onto its top side, and take away the paper that it's been sitting on to dehydrate – this side should be slightly damper than the other.

Spread fig paste evenly in a strip in the middle of the dough, then carefully fold in each side of the dough to the centre using the paper. Transfer to the fridge to set for 30 minutes, then cut into 6–8 rolls. The rolls will keep well in the fridge for up to 1 week.

Tiramisu

Who doesn't love tiramisu? So many of our friends wanted us to recreate a raw version of this classic. There are many different takes on this traditional Italian dessert, but the lady fingers and the rich coffee flavour are paramount. Our tiramisu portions are square, free-standing and dangerously delicious.

2 tbsp fresh organic coffee
   beans, plus extra to decorate
2 tbsp cacao nibs

For the base
80g (1 cup) walnuts
145g (1 cup) almonds
125g (1 cup) pitted dates,
   soaked until soft
20g (¼ cup) cacao powder
65ml (¼ cup) almond milk
35g (¼ cup) coconut sugar

For the ladyfinger logs
70g (1 cup) gluten-free oats
125g (1 cup) pitted dates,
   soaked until soft
2 tbsp cold-brew coffee
   (see page 183)
1 tsp vanilla powder
1 tbsp maca powder

For the cream
260g (2 cups) cashews
170g (½ cup) rice malt syrup
   or alternative liquid
   natural sweetener
50g (¼ cup) coconut oil, melted
1 tsp vanilla powder
1 tsp lucuma powder
125ml (½ cup) filtered water

MAKES 4–6 SQUARES

Line a 15cm square baking tin with baking paper. Blend the coffee beans and cacao nibs in a high-powered food processor on high to create a semi-fine dust, then set aside in a small bowl.

To make the base, grind the nuts in the food processor until they become a fine flour. Add all the remaining ingredients and mix until well combined and the mixture forms a sticky ball. Press the mixture evenly into the tin and set aside. Clean out the bowl of the food processor.

To make the ladyfingers, grind the oats to a flour in the clean food processor on a high speed, then add the dates and blend again until smooth. Add the remaining ingredients and roll the mixture into 4–6 fat fingers, then place the fingers on a lined baking sheet or plate, pressing them down gently. Place in the fridge for 1–2 hours until firm and set.

For the cream layer, blend all the ingredients until the mixture is smooth, adding the water gradually (you might not need it all). Spread a quarter of the cream on top of the nut mixture, smooth it over and let it set in the fridge or freezer for 30 minutes.

When the ladyfingers are firm, place them lengthways on top of the first cream layer, then pour the rest of the cream on top. Set in the fridge overnight. If the pudding mixture is still very soft the next day, place it in the freezer for 30 minutes before serving. Remove the tiramisu from the tin, cut with a sharp knife into 4–6 rectangular servings and dust with cacao powder and a sprinkle of the ground coffee bean and cacao nib mixture.

raw cake

raw treats

From the Freezer

Chapter 4

It's impossible to go wrong with these frozen treats. They're perfect for stockpiling and revisiting any time you get the urge. We stock our freezer with these the way Grandma used to fill the drop freezer in the garage; relentlessly. Refreshing, indulgent, light or rich, there's something in here for every moment of need and the best thing is that they're absolutely 100 per cent mistake-proof. We've always been suckers for collecting lollipop moulds – it takes us back to our youth. You can do the same or stick to the standard moulds that you can buy from supermarkets – it's totally up to you.

Sencha & Almond Milk Pops

These Japanese-inspired creamy dream pops are hydrating and uplifting all at once. If you're struggling to get your hands on sencha, then use any other green tea you can find – the stronger the brew, the better.

For the cream layer

250ml (1 cup) homemade
  almond milk (for extra
  creaminess)
130g (1 cup) cashews, soaked
85g (¼ cup) rice malt syrup
  or alternative liquid
  natural sweetener

For the green tea layer

250ml (1 cup) strong brewed
  Sencha green tea (or matcha)
1 tbsp rice malt syrup or
  alternative liquid natural
  sweetener (optional)

MAKES 6–8 POPS

First make the cream layer. Put all the ingredients in a high-powered food processor and blend on high until smooth.

Pour the almond cream into the lolly moulds until each mould is half full. Place into the freezer for 2 hours or until frozen.

Once the brewed tea is cool and the cream layer is frozen, pour the tea (sweetened, if you wish) into the lolly moulds, pop in the lolly sticks and return to the freezer for a further 3 hours or overnight. Alternatively, you can pour your mixtures in thinner layers, creating stripes.

They will keep in the freezer for 2 weeks. To get the lollies out easily, place the bottoms of the moulds under warm running water to loosen them.

115

Strawberry & Schisandra Pops

Putting the 'pop' in ice pop, there's something undeniably cutesie about these fruity strawberry sensations. The recipe is endlessly versatile, too. Try replacing the strawberries with other berries such as raspberries, blackberries or blueberries, or go tropical with mango or pineapple.
(Pictured on pages 112-113.)

144g (1 cup) strawberries
1 x 400ml can coconut milk
1 tbsp maple syrup
1 tbsp schisandra
pinch of Himalayan salt
desiccated coconut, to decorate

MAKES 6—8 POPS

Place the strawberries in a high-powered food processor and blend on high until broken down and smooth, then add the remaining ingredients except for the coconut and blend again for 1 minute – the mixture might separate slightly, but this will just give the lollies a cute speckled appearance.

Sprinkle the desiccated coconut in the bottom half of the ice lolly moulds, pour in the strawberry mixture and insert the lolly sticks, then place in the freezer overnight.

They will keep in the freezer for 2 weeks. To get the lollies out easily, place the bottoms of the moulds under warm running water to loosen them.

Cacao Fudgsicles

These are perfect for the kids, but you're probably not going to want to share them. The perfect summer's day indulgence, these are Mini Milk's older, cooler, plant-based brother. *(Pictured on pages 112-113.)*

65g (½ cup) cashews, soaked either overnight in cool water or 1 hour in hot water, then drained
60g (½ cup) pitted dates, soaked until soft, then drained
1 x 400ml can coconut milk
40g (½ cup) cacao powder
2 tbsp coconut oil, melted
½ tsp vanilla powder
1 tbsp maca powder (optional)
raw buckwheat and cacao nibs, to decorate

MAKES 6—8 FUDGSICLES

Place the drained cashews in a high-powered food processor and blend on high until as fine as possible, then add the dates and blend together. Mix in all the remaining ingredients except for the buckwheat and cacao nibs until the mixture is creamy with no lumps. This should take only a couple of minutes. Sprinkle a few of the buckwheat and cacao nibs into the bottom of your lolly moulds.

Pour the fudge mix into the moulds, insert the lolly sticks and freeze overnight.

They will keep in the freezer for 2 weeks. To get the lollies out easily, place the bottoms of the moulds under warm running water to loosen them.

117

Tea Cucumber Detox Coolers

Daily detox soothers, these refreshing lollies are ideal for hydration. With the uplifting qualities of tea and cooling cucumber, these will clear brain fog and combat skin irritation as well as ageing.

1 medium cucumber, skinless and seedless
zest and juice of 1 lemon
500ml (2 cups) cold-brewed tea of your choice (we used lemongrass green tea)
1 tbsp rice malt syrup or alternative liquid natural sweetener (optional)
1 tbsp collagen powder (optional)

MAKES 6—8 LOLLIES

Place the cucumber in a high-powered food processor and pulse until roughly broken up but still very chunky. Add all the remaining ingredients and pulse until well combined.

Pour the mixture into your ice lolly moulds, insert the lolly sticks and freeze overnight.

They will keep in the freezer for 2 weeks. To get the lollies out easily, place the bottoms of the moulds under warm running water to loosen them.

118

Cold-brewed Teas
Try switching the flavour of cold-brewed tea: camomile, honeysuckle flower, nettle, lemon verbena leaf and peppermint all work beautifully.

from the freezer

Mint Chocolate Ice Lollies

One for the boys, this creamy peppermint flavour is ideal for a mid-week after-dinner clean treat. We find the hydrating qualities of spirulina so refreshing in this recipe, and with the addition of the emotionally uplifting, heart-opening qualities of raw cacao it's an all-round body and energy booster. You can find fresh mint in most supermarkets, but if you have the chance to use mint you've grown yourself you'll be blown away.

130g (1 cup) cashews, soaked
    for 1 hour then drained
190ml (¾ cup) almond milk
    or other nut milk
2 fresh mint sprigs, leaves only
8-10 drops food-grade
    peppermint essential oil
85g (¼ cup) rice malt syrup
¾ tsp spirulina powder
1-2 tbsp cacao nibs
Raw Chocolate
    (see page 26), for dipping

MAKES 6–8 LOLLIES

Place the cashews and almond milk in a high-powered food processor and blend on high until smooth. Add the remaining ingredients except the cacao nibs and chocolate and blend on high again until the mint is completely broken down. Stir in the cacao nibs to evenly distribute. Pour into ice lolly moulds, insert the lolly sticks and place in the freezer overnight.

Remove the lollies from their moulds – run a little warm water on the bottoms of the moulds if they are hard to get out. To finish, dip the lollies in the Raw Chocolate and place each on a sheet of baking paper set on a baking tray that will fit in your freezer. Once all the lollies are dipped, return them to the freezer again for 5–10 minutes for the chocolate to set.

raw cake

Purple
Cream

We're a huge fan of acai bowls. We actually fell in love with them in Copenhagen, so when we created this recipe we wanted something similar but a frozen version that could be served with an evening meal as a pudding and not just for breakfast.

200g (2 cups) frozen
   blueberries
130g (1 cup) cashews,
   soaked for 2 hours until soft,
   then drained
1 x 400ml can coconut
   milk (place in the fridge
   overnight, then use the top
   layer of cream only)
85g (¼ cup) maple syrup
   or coconut syrup
30g (¼ cup) coconut sugar
1 tbsp acai powder
¼ tsp vanilla powder
   or seeds of 1 vanilla pod
pinch of Himalayan salt

SERVES 2—4

Place all the ingredients in a high-powered food processor and blend on high until smooth, then pour into a freezerproof container or ice-lolly moulds, cover, and freeze for 2–3 hours or overnight.

Once the mixture is scoopable, scoop and serve. If it is hard, blend it again in the food processor before serving.

123

Cookie
Dough
Ice Cream

Inspired by everyone's favourite Ben & Jerry's flavour, watch the whole bowl of this naturally, creamy nuttiness disappear as you hunker down for a Saturday night on the sofa with this beauty. Every bit as delicious as the original, this is Nature's way of showing how much it loves you.

For the ice cream

65g (½ cup) cashews, soaked
  and drained
½ x 400ml can coconut
  milk (place in the fridge
  overnight, then only use
  the top layer of cream)
125ml (½ cup) homemade
  almond milk (important
  that it's homemade due to
  the creaminess and higher
  content of almonds)
30g (¼ cup) coconut sugar
½ tsp vanilla powder
pinch of salt

For the cookie dough pieces

65g (½ cup) cashews
60g (½ cup) pitted
  Medjool dates
30g (¼ cup) coconut sugar
¼ tsp vanilla powder
pinch of Himalayan salt

124

SERVES 2

First make the ice cream. Scoop out the layer of cream on the top of the watery coconut milk, and place it in a high-speed food processor with all the remaining ingredients, then blend on high until smooth. Transfer to a medium freezerproof container, put the lid on and freeze for 2–3 hours until the mixture is solid. Clean out the bowl of the food processor.

For the cookie dough pieces, blend all the ingredients together in the clean food processor. Scrape the sides down a couple of times and re-blend until gooey and fine. Spread the mixture out into a thin layer on a baking sheet and leave in the fridge for 1–2 hours until chilled and less sticky. Roll into small uneven balls.

When ready to eat, remove the ice cream from the freezer, break up the block, put it back into the food processor and pulse until it breaks up and has a creamy texture. Try not to over-mix here. Add the cookie dough balls to the ice cream and serve immediately.

from the freezer

Sea Green Sorbet

Sea green sorbet is basically edible algae and vegetables masquerading deliciously as a sweet sorbet. The addition of hydrating apple and kiwi boosts its vitamin C content and gives the sorbet a tantalizingly tart flavour. It's also surprisingly great before bed thanks to the magnesium in spinach. The kids will never know.

1 avocado, stoned, cubed
   and frozen
2 apples, cored and quartered
2 kiwis, skinned and quartered
2 handfuls of fresh spinach
   (about 60g/2 cups)
1 lime, peeled
½ tbsp spirulina powder
½ tbsp chlorella powder
½ tbsp wheatgrass powder

SERVES 2—4

Place all the ingredients, except the powders in a high-powered food processor and blend on high for 3–5 minutes until smooth. Add the powders (if you don't have them all, add the ones you have or perhaps a green powder blend) and blend until as smooth as possible.

Transfer to a freezerproof container or ice-cube trays, cover, then freeze for 4–6 hours. Remove from the freezer and re-blend the frozen mixture briefly in a food processor to break it up. When it becomes an icy sorbet texture, stop blending and serve straight away.

126

Kiwi
A great source of vitamin C, tangy, succulent kiwis also contain a protein-dissolving enzyme that can help with digestion after a large meal.

Cinnamon Coffee Cream

A deviously delicious blend of two grown-up flavours, the uplifting aroma of coffee and the grounding homeliness of cinnamon are a harmonious duo. There's nothing Bridget Jones about eating an entire bowl of this.

250ml (1 cup) strong
  cold-brew coffee
  (see page 183)
65g (½ cup) cashews, soaked
  and drained
125ml (½ cup) almond milk
  or other non-dairy milk
¼ tsp ground cinnamon
2 tbsp maple syrup

SERVES 2

Place all the ingredients in a high-powered food processor and blend on high until the mixture becomes creamy. If it looks too watery, add some more cashews to thicken it up.

Place into ice-cube trays or a freezable container, cover, then freeze for 4–5 hours or preferably overnight.

Remove from the freezer, return the frozen mixture to the food processor and blend until it becomes sorbet-like. Serve straight away.

127

Lemon, Mango & Ginger Ginseng Sorbet

Zesty and uplifting, with the delicate sweetness of mango and a little rhizome kick, we sometimes can't believe that this sorbet is nutritious as well as delicious. With the detoxifying qualities of lemon and the anti-inflammatory qualities of ginger, you'll certainly have a spring in your step after eating this.

zest and juice of 1 lemon

5cm piece of fresh root
   ginger, peeled

1 large mango, peeled and
   destoned

3 tbsp rice malt syrup
   or alternative liquid
   natural sweetener

60ml (¼ cup) filtered water

1 tsp Siberian ginseng
   (optional)

desiccated or flaked coconut,
   to garnish

SERVES 2—4

Place all the ingredients except for the coconut in a high-powered food processor and blend on high, then pour into a medium freezerproof container or ice-cube trays, cover, then freeze for 3–4 hours until fully frozen.

Take the sorbet out of the freezer and place in the food processor again, then blend or pulse the frozen mixture for a few seconds until the mixture becomes sorbet-like. Serve straight away, garnished with desiccated or flaked coconut.

from the freezer

raw cake

Cherry,
Lucuma
& Banana
Ice Cream

In this recipe, banana ice cream gets a cheeky cherry twist. It's best to make this using cherries only when they are in season, otherwise you'll find that the fruit won't be as tasty and the sweet cherry flavour won't come through. If cherries are not in season, you can easily create this recipe with many other fruits, including blueberries, strawberries, raspberries or figs. Try experimenting with your favourites.

335g (1½ cups) fresh cherries,
    halved and pitted
1 tbsp coconut syrup
2½ bananas, sliced and frozen
1 tbsp lucuma powder

SERVES 2

Place a third of the cherries in a high-powered food processor with the coconut syrup and pulse until roughly broken up. Set aside in a bowl or cup.

Place the frozen bananas in the food processor with another third of the cherries and the lucuma and blend for 3–4 minutes on high. The blender might struggle for the first 30 seconds, but then the banana will break up into pieces and eventually will become smooth. Blend until everything is smooth, but don't over-blend or the banana will start to melt. (This should take 2–3 minutes depending on your machine.)

Layer the blended cherries, banana ice cream and the remaining fresh cherries in cups or bowls and serve straight away.

131

Raw Cheesecakes

Chapter 5

Cheesecakes are the crowning glory of raw desserts and the holy grail for those who make them. They are what we're most known for and they took us an age to master. If we had a penny for every soggy cheesecake we had to pour into a glass and serve as a mousse, we'd be rich. No doubt, these beauties are tricky, but don't let this put you off – like all of the best things in life you'll need to practise to make them showstoppingly impressive, but once you get there it'll be more than worth it, honestly. Of course, there is always the chance you'll get it first time and it was just us who couldn't quite get our heads around it, but you won't know until you try!

134

White Chocolate Raspberry Cheesecake

A real centrepiece, this cheesecake will be the star of the show at any dinner party. We love that the fresh raspberries are visible throughout the cake and the luxurious beetroot base. For a herby, botanical look sprinkle fresh amaranth on top. Present this cake with pride, it's a beauty. *(Pictured on pages 132-133.)*

For the base

130g (1 cup) cashews

75g (1 cup) desiccated coconut

2 tbsp beetroot powder
(or use beetroot juice
if you don't have powder)

3 tbsp rice malt syrup

pinch of Himalayan salt

For the filling

260g (2 cups) cashews,
soaked for 1-2 hours

90g (1 cup) fresh diced
coconut flesh

340g (1 cup) rice malt syrup

60ml (¼ cup) almond milk

3 tbsp lemon juice

2 tbsp cacao butter

1 tsp vanilla powder

100g (½ cup) coconut oil

20-25 fresh raspberries, plus
extra to decorate

edible flowers, to decorate

cashew cream, to decorate
(see page 80)

SERVES 12—16

Line a 20cm round springform cake tin with baking paper.

For the base, place the cashews and coconut in a high-powered food processor and blend on high until fine, then add the remaining ingredients and blend again until well combined. Press the base into the bottom of the cake tin and clean out the bowl of the food processor.

For the filling, add the soaked cashews to the clean food processor or a high-speed blender (for extra smoothness) and blend on high until well broken up. Add the coconut flesh and blend again, making sure they have combined. Add the remaining ingredients except for the raspberries, flowers and cashew cream, and blend for a further 2 minutes until the mixture has a smooth, creamy consistency.

Place the raspberries in the tin on top of the base and pour the cheesecake mix on top of them, making sure they're covered. Place in the fridge overnight or the freezer for 2–3 hours to set. It will keep well (undecorated) in the fridge for up to 3 days.

Decorate with extra cashew cream piped onto the top, and raspberries and edible flowers.

135

raw cheesecakes

Nut-free Coconut & Lime Mousse Cake

Most raw cheesecakes rely on nuts, but this light and airy variation doesn't need them. Fresh and uplifting, the tart lime works in harmony with the soothing creamy coconut to create a delicate yet decadent dessert. Cut into cubes in our signature style and you're looking at a winner.

For the base

15g (¼ cup) gluten-free oats

45g (¼ cup) raw buckwheat

75g (1 cup) desiccated coconut

zest of 1 lime

1 tbsp golden linseed

1 tbsp tulsi (optional)

generous pinch of salt

3 tbsp rice malt syrup

For the filling

2½ x 160ml cans coconut cream

75g (1 cup) desiccated coconut, ground fine like flour, plus extra to decorate

100g (½ cup) coconut oil

255g (¾ cup) rice malt syrup

1 tbsp cacao butter

3 tbsp lime juice

zest of ½ lime

pinch of Himalayan salt

thin slices of fresh lime, desiccated coconut and bee pollen, to decorate (see note on safe use of bee pollen on p181)

SERVES 6—8

Line a 15cm square baking tin with baking paper.

For the base, place all the ingredients except the rice malt syrup in a high-powered food processor and pulse until broken up roughly. Add the rice malt syrup and blend until medium-fine and well combined, then press into the baking tin. Clean out the bowl of the food processor.

Add all the ingredients for the filling into the clean food processor and pulse until everything is well combined and smooth, making sure the desiccated coconut has combined well. Pour the mixture, which should be quite runny, into the tin and quickly transfer to the freezer for 2–3 hours until well set.

If the cake is rock solid when you take it out, let it thaw for 20–30 minutes before serving. It will keep in the fridge for up to 3 days.

To serve, cut into 6–8 cubes and decorate with lime slices, desiccated coconut and bee pollen.

136

raw cheesecakes

Ginger Chai Latte Cheesecake

When we first came up with this recipe we wanted to use some of our favourite, more sophisticated flavours. Warming ginger, cardamom, cinnamon, nutmeg and allspice make this cheesecake a feast for the soul. If chai lattes are your go-to beverage, this dessert is the one for you.

SERVES 8–12

For the base
130g (1 cup) cashews
40g (½ cup) walnuts
4cm ginger, peeled and chopped
65g (½ cup) coconut sugar
125g (1 cup) pitted dates

For the filling
325g (2½ cups) cashews, soaked
   for 1 hour or until soft
200g (1 cup) coconut oil, melted
340g (1 cup) rice syrup
4cm ginger, peeled and chopped
seeds from 10-14 cardamom pods
½ tsp each of ground cinnamon,
   allspice and grated nutmeg
¼ tsp vanilla powder
pinch of ground black pepper

For the crumble topping
65g (½ cup) cashews
40g (½ cup) walnuts
½ tsp ground cinnamon
seeds from 6 cardamom pods
pinch of ground black pepper

For the toffee drizzle
60g (½ cup) pitted soft dates
170g (½ cup) maple syrup
1 tbsp tahini paste
1 tbsp maca powder
¼ tsp vanilla powder
pinch of Himalayan salt

Line a 20cm round cake tin or pie dish with baking paper.

To make the base, place the nuts in a high-powered blender and blend roughly, then add the ginger, coconut sugar and dates and blend until well combined. Press into the tin or dish.

For the filling, blend the cashews in a high-powered food processor until they are as smooth as possible, add the remaining ingredients and blend on high until everything has broken down and become smooth. Pour on top of the base and clean out the bowl of the food processor.

For the crumble topping, add all the ingredients to the clean food processor and pulse slowly so that everything combines but still remains very coarse. Pour this on top of the filling and press down gently. Place the tin in the fridge overnight or into the freezer for 2–4 hours to set. Clean out the bowl of the food processor.

Meanwhile, make the toffee drizzle. Drain the dates and place in the clean food processor, blend on high until broken up, then add all the other ingredients and blend again until smooth. If the mixture is quite thick, add 1–2 tablespoons of warm water so that it will drizzle easily.

When you're ready to eat, remove the cheesecake from the freezer, drizzle the toffee sauce on top and serve.

Macadamia Cinnamon Cheesecake

We love macadamias because they are a great alternative or addition to cashews when making raw cheesecakes. They are well worth the high price tag for their creamy texture and flavour. The sophisticated flavours in this cheesecake were inspired by figs we foraged in Ibiza.

For the base

145g (1 cup) dried figs,
　　soaked for 30 minutes, plus
　　220g (1½ cups) dried figs
70g (1 cup) almonds
2 tbsp rice malt syrup
1 tbsp maca powder (optional)
pinch of salt
20g (¼ cup) cacao powder
2 tbsp coconut sugar
dried coconut flakes, to decorate

For the filling

195g (1½ cups) cashews,
　　soaked for 2 hours in cold
　　water or 30 minutes in warm
65g (½ cup) macadamias,
　　soaked as cashews
60g (¼ cup) coconut milk
1 tbsp cacao butter, melted
170g (½ cup) rice malt syrup
50g (¼ cup) coconut oil
60ml (¼ cup) lemon juice
2 tbsp ground cinnamon,
　　plus extra to taste (optional)

SERVES 6—8

Line a 15cm square baking tin with baking paper.

To make the base, place the 145g (1 cup) soaked figs in a high-powered food processor and blend on high until broken up, then add all the remaining ingredients except the extra figs, cacao powder, coconut sugar and coconut flakes. Blend again and add the cacao in last. Press the mixture into the baking tin and clean out the bowl of the food processor.

Next, add the extra figs and coconut sugar to the clean food processor and blend until rough, then crumble this on top of your base and set aside.

For the filling, drain the nuts and add to the clean food processor. Blend on high until as fine as possible before incorporating the rest of the ingredients, then blend until there are no lumps. Add more cinnamon, if needed.

When ready, pour the filling on top of the base, making sure it is all covered. Put in the fridge overnight or the freezer for 2–3 hours until set. Decorate with some coconut flakes.

139

Toffee Cacao Cheesecake

This super-indulgent, velvety cheesecake with brownie pieces enveloped in toffee and chocolate is guaranteed to fulfil the most insatiable of chocolate cravings. With maca, chaga, cacao nibs and cacao powder, it's a real slice of the nutritionally delicious.

For the base

50g (½ cup) pecans
60g (½ cup) hazelnuts
125g (1 cup) pitted dates
25g (¼ cup) cacao nibs
1 tbsp maca powder
1 tbsp chaga powder
½ tsp salt

For the filling

260g (2 cups) cashews, soaked and drained
125ml (½ cup) coconut milk
240g (1 cup) date paste
100g (½ cup) coconut oil
120g (½ cup) almond butter
170g (½ cup) rice malt syrup
½ tsp salt
1 tbsp maca powder
1 tsp vanilla powder
40g (½ cup) cacao powder

Nut-free Double Chocolate Brownies (see page 108)
date paste and chopped chocolate chunks, to serve (optional)

SERVES 8—12

Line a 20cm round springform cake tin with baking paper.

Make the base by blending the pecans and hazelnuts in a high-powered food processor on high until ground. Add the remaining base ingredients and blend until well combined and slightly gooey. Press into the cake tin and clean out the bowl of the food processor.

For the filling, add the cashews to the clean food processor and blitz for 1–2 minutes until very smooth. Add the coconut milk and pulse, before adding the rest of the ingredients. Mix until thick and smooth.

Scatter pieces of brownie over the base layer, then pour in the cashew filling and place in the fridge for 3–4 hours or overnight to set.

For a special occasion, pipe some date paste around the top, and decorate with chocolate chunks and edible flower petals.

141

Hawaiian Cheesecake

An exotic twist on traditional cheesecake, this Hawaii-inspired dream will take you to the Pacific and back in a single mouthful. The goji berries in the base are a particularly special touch, and who can resist fresh pineapple?

For the base
65g (½ cup) cashews
70g (½ cup) almonds
30g (¼ cup) goji berries
85g (¼ cup) rice malt syrup
1 tbsp maca powder
pinch of salt
125g (1 cup) pitted dates,
   soaked if very hard

For the cheesecake layer
390g (3 cups) cashews
300g (1½ cups) fresh
   diced pineapple
425g (1¼ cups) rice malt
   syrup or maple syrup
200g (1 cup) coconut oil, melted
35g (½ cup) desiccated coconut
1 tbsp vanilla powder

For the pineapple sorbet
400g (2 cups) fresh diced,
   pineapple, plus extra for
   the topping
85g (¼ cup) rice malt syrup
100g (½ cup) coconut oil,
   melted

SERVES 8—12

Line a 20cm round springform cake tin with baking paper.

For the base, place all the ingredients except the dates in a high-powered food processor and blend on high briefly to combine, then add the dates and blend again until well combined. Press the mixture into the cake tin.

For the cheesecake layer, place the cashews in a high-powered blender and blend on high until they are as smooth as possible. Add all the remaining cheesecake layer ingredients and blend again on high for a few minutes until the mixture is smooth. Pour half the mix on top of the base and place in the freezer to set.

Meanwhile, make the pineapple sorbet. Blend the pineapple and syrup together in a blender, pour into a fine sieve and drain all the excess juice. Blend again with the coconut oil and place into a bowl and put in the fridge for 30 minutes. When the sorbet is slightly set, spoon it over the first cheesecake layer, smooth down, then top with the rest of the cheesecake mix.

Place in the freezer for 2 hours or the fridge overnight to set, decorate with the extra diced pineapple on top and serve chilled.

Cacao Mint Layer Cake

Adapted from one of our best sellers, this triple-decker delight is the perfect dinner party serve. With cacao, spirulina and wheatgrass, it packs a serious superfood punch while the peppermint oil cuts through the sweetness refreshingly.

For the base

70g (½ cup) almonds

40g (½ cup) walnuts

115g (1½ cups) desiccated coconut

125g (1 cup) pitted Medjool dates (if not Medjool, soak to soften)

20g (¼ cup) cacao powder

85g (¼ cup) rice malt syrup

¼ tsp Himalayan salt

For the mint filling

195g (1½ cups) cashews, soaked for 2 hours and drained

300g (1½ cups) coconut oil, melted

1 tbsp spirulina powder

1 tbsp wheatgrass powder

10-15 drops peppermint oil

2 tbsp rice syrup

For the chocolate frosting

65g (½ cup) cashews, soaked for 2 hours and drained

200g (1 cup) coconut oil, melted

170g (½ cup) rice malt syrup

20g (¼ cup) cacao powder, plus extra (optional)

1 tbsp cacao butter, melted

1 tsp vanilla powder

SERVES 8—12

Line a 20cm round springform cake tin with baking paper.

First make the base. Place the nuts in a high-powered food processor and blitz until roughly ground, then add the remaining ingredients and blend on high until well combined. Press into the cake tin and clean out the bowl of the food processor.

Next, make the mint filling. Blend the cashews in the clean food processor on high until as smooth as possible. Add the remaining ingredients and blend again on high. Pour over the base and place in the freezer for 20–30 minutes until set. Clean out the bowl of the food processor.

For the frosting, blend the cashews in the clean food processor on high until as smooth as possible, then add the remaining ingredients, blitzing until smooth. If the mixture is too oily, add some extra cacao powder; if it's too rough and not shiny, add a small splash of water.

Pour on top of your set mint layer and place in the fridge overnight or the freezer for 2–4 hours. Enjoy chilled. It will keep well for up to 5 days in the fridge.

143

raw cheesecakes

raw cake

Chocolate Orange Rocky Road Cake

Channelling our inner Dawn French, this cake isn't Terry's... it's ours. Adding pieces of our vegan Rocky Road to this flavoursome cake takes it to the next level, but if you prefer to keep things simple you can always leave them out.

For the base

130g (1 cup) cashews

100g (1 cup) pecans

75g (1 cup) desiccated coconut

20g (¼ cup) cacao powder

125g (1 cup) pitted Medjool
  dates, or soaked until soft

1 tbsp maca powder (optional)

pinch of salt

small chunks of Rocky Road
  (see page 96)

For the filling

390g (3 cups) cashews,
  soaked for 2 hours

300g (1½ cups) coconut
  oil, melted

60g (¾ cup) cacao powder,
  plus extra (optional)

340g (1 cup) rice malt syrup

250ml (1 cup) freshly
  squeezed orange juice,
  plus extra (optional)

zest of 1 orange

pinch of Himalayan salt

dehydrated orange pieces,
  cacao nibs, and edible flowers
  or Dark Chocolate Truffles
  (see page 101), to decorate

SERVES 8–12

Line a 20cm round springform cake tin with baking paper.

For the base, place the nuts and desiccated coconut in a high-powered food processor and blend on high until roughly broken up. Add the remaining ingredients, except the Rocky Road, and blend on high until well combined. Press into the bottom of the cake tin.

Crumble a few handfuls of the Rocky Road in small chunks over the base.

For the filling, drain the cashews, place them in a high-powered blender or food processor and blend until they are broken down and fine. Add the remaining ingredients and blend for up to 5 minutes depending on your machine, until the mixture is completely smooth. If it looks too runny, add some extra cacao powder; if it's too thick, add some more orange juice.

Pour the filling over the Rocky Road pieces, then place the tin in the fridge overnight or in the freezer for 3–4 hours to set. Keep in the fridge until ready to serve.

Decorate with dehydrated orange pieces, cacao nibs and edible flowers or Dark Chocolate Truffles.

145

raw cheesecakes

Blueberry Lemon Swirl Cheesecake

Coloured swirls are the *pièce de résistance* of the cheesecake world. We used to be in awe of them before we learned how to create them ourselves. Our first attempt was blotchy but not without beauty. Stick with it – if you don't get it right first time, you can refine your technique with each attempt! *(Pictured on pages 146–147.)*

For the base

130g (1 cup) cashews

50g (½ cup) pecans

60g (½ cup) pitted soft dates

2 tbsp rice malt syrup
    or alternative liquid
    natural sweetener

1 tbsp maca powder (optional)

pinch of Himalayan salt

For the filling and topping

60g (¾ cup) desiccated
    coconut

390g (3 cups) cashews, soaked
    in warm water for 2 hours
    then drained

340g (1 cup) rice malt syrup
    or alternative liquid
    natural sweetener

200g (1 cup) coconut oil, melted

125ml (½ cup) lemon juice

zest of 1 lemon,
    plus extra to decorate

½ tsp turmeric powder

200g (2 cups) fresh or
    frozen blueberries

edible flowers and coconut
    flakes, to decorate

SERVES 8–12

Line a 20cm round springform cake tin with baking paper.

For the base, place the nuts in a high-powered food processor and blend on high until coarsely ground, then combine with the remaining ingredients until well mixed. Press into the cake tin.

For the filling, place the coconut in a high-powered blender and blend on high until fine, then add the cashews, syrup and coconut oil and blend again until the mixture is as smooth as possible, scraping down the sides to incorporate all the mixture. Transfer half the mixture to a bowl and set aside. Add the lemon juice, zest and turmeric to the mixture left in the blender and blend until smooth. Taste, and add more lemon juice if it needs more flavour, and more sweetener if it's too tart. Pour into a second bowl, setting aside a few tablespoons of this lemon cream in a piping bag to chill for later. Add the other half of the mixture to the blender with the blueberries. Blend until combined and add more sweetener if needed. Pour it back into the bowl.

Spoon equal-sized dollops of the purple mixture and the yellow mixture at random onto the cake base, alternating between colours, until you have used it all up. Wiggle the tin from side to side to settle the mixture, and swirl through the mix using a knife or chopstick, to create a pattern. Transfer to the fridge overnight or the freezer for 3–4 hours until firm. Remove from the tin and decorate with the lemon cream, edible flowers, coconut flakes and lemon zest. Chill until ready to serve.

148

raw cake

Peanut Butter Cheesecake

Don't let the simplicity of this recipe fool you. When you've made it once, you'll keep dreaming about it until you make it again. We first made this for a peanut butter-obsessed friend and now we make it at least once a month!

For the base

35g (¼ cup) raw
   unsalted peanuts
35g (¼ cup) almonds
125g (1 cup) dates, Medjool
   or soaked until soft, not wet
2 tbsp golden linseed
½ tbsp peanut butter
pinch of Himalayan salt

For the filling

3 large or 4 small bananas
260g (1 cup) peanut butter
85g (¼ cup) rice malt syrup
50g (¼ cup) coconut oil,
   melted
1 tbsp maca powder
¼ tsp vanilla powder

SERVES 8—12

Line a 20cm round springform cake tin with baking paper.

For the base, place the peanuts and almonds in a high-powered food processor and blend on high for a few seconds to roughly break them down. Add the remaining ingredients and blend until the mixture is well combined and slightly sticky. Press into the base of the cake tin.

For the filling, put the bananas and peanut butter into the food processor and blend until combined. Blend together with the rest of the ingredients until the mixture is smooth. Pour the filling on top of the base and put in the fridge for 3–4 hours to set.

149

Chapter 6

As perfect sharers, these are what we turn to when we're supposed to be sharing. If 'hostess with the mostess' is the accolade you're aiming for, these are for you. We whip these up when we want people to believe we're grown-ups – and the trick works every time.

Lemon Baobab Curd Pie

Our take on a lemon meringue pie, the baobab in this complements the zesty lemon flavours seamlessly. This is an absolute crowd pleaser and a centrepiece to any dinner party table. *(Pictured on pages 150-151.)*

For the base
75g (1 cup) desiccated coconut

65g (½ cup) cashews

zest of 1 lemon

3 tbsp rice malt syrup

1 tbsp tahini paste

1 tbsp lucuma powder (optional)

For the lemon filling
65g (½ cup) cashews,
 soaked for 1–2 hours
 and drained

125ml (½ cup) lemon juice

50g (¼ cup) coconut oil

1 x 400ml can coconut milk
 (place in the fridge overnight,
 then only use the top layer of
 cream)

zest of 1 lemon, plus extra
 to serve

3 tbsp chia seeds, cover in
 water and soak for 20 minutes
 until they become gel

½ tbsp baobab powder

85g (¼ cup) rice malt syrup

1 tsp turmeric powder

pinch of salt

For the coconut cream whip
2 x 400ml cans coconut milk
 (place in the fridge overnight,
 then only use the top layer of
 cream)

2 tbsp rice malt syrup

SERVES 8—12

Line a 20cm pie tin with baking paper.

For the base, place the coconut and cashews in a high-powered food processor and blend on high until roughly broken up. Add the remaining ingredients with 2 tablespoons of water and blend again until the mixture is fine and well combined. Press the base mixture into the pie tin, pressing it up the sides.

For the filling, place the drained cashews, lemon juice and coconut oil in a high-powered blender and blend on high until the cashews have broken down as much as possible. Scoop out the layer of cream on the top of the coconut milk, and add it with the remaining ingredients. Blend again on high until the mixture is smooth and creamy. Pour into the base and put the pie in the fridge for 3–4 hours or overnight to set.

Finally, make the coconut cream. Scoop out the layer of cream on the top of the watery coconut milk, then add it and the syrup to the food processor and blend on high until the cream becomes smooth and lump-free. Don't over-mix or the cream will become too sloppy.

Spoon the coconut cream on top of the meringue pie and keep in the fridge until ready to serve, then slice and garnish with the extra lemon zest.

153

Maple Maca Pecan Pie

Maple maca pecan pie – try saying that with your mouth full! Straight out of the United States with a superfood booster, this won't stay in your fridge for long.

For the crust

200g (2 cups) pecans

125g (1 cup) dates, soaked for 30 minutes or until soft if hard

2 tbsp tahini paste

2 tbsp maca powder

generous pinch of salt

For the filling

200g (2 cups) pecans, plus extra, halved, to decorate

500g (4 cups) dates, soaked for 30 minutes or until soft if hard

150g (¾ cup) coconut oil, melted

125ml (½ cup) almond milk

85g (¼ cup) maple syrup

2 tbsp maca powder

½ tsp ground cinnamon

generous pinch of salt

SERVES 8—12

Line a 20cm round pie dish with baking paper.

First make the crust. Place the pecans in a high-powered blender and blitz on high until they are roughly chopped. Add all the remaining ingredients and blend until well combined. If the mixture doesn't sticks together when pressed, add in 1 tablespoon of water. Press into the pie dish, pressing it up the sides.

For the filling, blend the pecans in the blender or a clean food processor until they are as fine as possible. Add the dates and blend again. Throw in the remaining ingredients and blitz again on high until all are well combined. Stop and scrape down the sides a few times to make sure the mixture is as smooth as possible.

Scoop the filling over the base and flatten down using a spatula. Press the pecan halves into the top to decorate. Leave in the fridge for at least 2 hours before removing from the pie dish and serving.

154

tarts, pies & pudding pots

raw cake

Salted Chocolate Chickpea Torte

This might sound a little unusual, but it was love at first bite for us. Chickpeas become smooth and gooey when blended and this protein-rich dessert is wonderfully dense, rich and sumptuous. No one will believe it's made of super-nutritious soaked chickpeas.

For the base

130g (1 cup) cashews

70g (½ cup) Brazil nuts

35g (¼ cup) coconut sugar

seeds of ½ vanilla pod or
    ½ tsp vanilla powder

3 tbsp raw cacao powder

pinch of Himalayan salt

125g (1 cup) pitted Medjool
    dates, or harder dates soaked
    for 30 minutes until soft

For the filling

480g (2 cups) raw chickpeas,
    soaked for 24 hours and rinsed

35g (¼ cup) coconut sugar

170g (½ cup) rice malt syrup
    or maple syrup

60g (½ cup) pitted Medjool
    dates, or harder dates soaked
    for 30 minutes until soft

20g (¼ cup) raw cacao powder

2 tbsp almond or other nut milk

seeds of 1½ vanilla pods,
    or 1 tsp vanilla powder

¼ tsp Himalayan salt

fresh cornflower petals, to
    garnish (optional)

SERVES 8–12

Line a 20cm round tart tin with baking paper.

First, make the base. Place the nuts in a high-powered food processor and blend on high until they are finely ground. Add the coconut sugar, vanilla, cacao and salt and blend again until they are combined. Add in the dates last and keep blending until the mixture sticks together well. If it is too crumbly, then add a tablespoon of water to help bind it. Press into the tart tin and clean out the bowl of the food processor.

For the filling, place all the ingredients in the clean food processor and blend on high for 5–8 minutes. Keep blending until the mixture becomes silky smooth and is not grainy any more. Pour the mixture into the base, spreading it out evenly, and put in the fridge for 1–2 hours to set. Serve chilled.

We like to finish our torte by decorating it with fresh cornflower petals for an extra flourish.

NOTE: If you can't get hold of raw chickpeas, then canned will work perfectly for this recipe, but do bear in mind that they have been cooked.

157

raw cake

Banana Lucuma Pies

Lucuma's nutritional benefits plus its biscuity flavour make this banana pie everything you are imagining and more. Even pictures don't do it justice. Rich in magnesium and potassium from the bananas, this is grounding, relaxing and delicious.

For the crust

195g (1½ cups) cashews,
    plus extra, chopped, to serve
110g (1½ cups)
    desiccated coconut
2 tbsp lucuma
generous pinch of salt

For the filling

3 large bananas, 2½ for the
    filling, ½ sliced to decorate
125ml (½ cup) coconut milk
240g (½ cup) date paste
100g (½ cup) coconut oil
1 tbsp lemon juice
½ tsp vanilla powder
2 tbsp lucuma
2 pinches of salt

For the caramel sauce

125g (1 cup) pitted dates,
    (soaked for 10 minutes
    in warm water, or 1 hour
    in cold water if hard)
125ml (½ cup) water
60g (¼ cup) almond butter
1 tbsp rice malt syrup
    or alternative liquid
    natural sweetener
½ tsp vanilla powder
generous pinch of salt

MAKES 4 PIES

If necessary (if your 4 tart tins – we use 8cm mini fluted tart tins – don't have removable bases), line the tins with pieces of baking paper that come up the sides of the tins, so that you can remove the pies easily.

For the crust, place the cashews in a high-powered blender and blend on high until broken up, then add the remaining ingredients with 1 tablespoon of water and mix until semi-fine (ideally you want a few chunks remaining). Press the mixture into your mini tins, pressing it up the fluted sides. Put in the fridge while you make the filling. Clean the blender.

For the filling, place the bananas and coconut milk in the blender and blend on high until smooth, then add the remaining filling ingredients and blend again, making sure your mixture is lovely and fine. Pour evenly into the tins and freeze for 30 minutes until set. Clean the blender.

For the caramel sauce, blend the dates with the water in a blender until combined. Add everything else and blend for 2–3 minutes making sure the mixture is as smooth as possible and pourable. If not, add some more water.

Take the pies out of the freezer and pop them out of the tins. Place the banana slices on top of each, drizzle with the caramel sauce and sprinkle with some chopped nuts. Voila!

159

Sticky Toffee Apple Pie

We first made this for a friend's birthday party and they just stopped short of calling us liars when we told them what it was made from. It's one of those recipes that people just can't believe is natural – a sticky, indulgent, autumnal-flavoured favourite.

For the base
260g (2 cups) cashews
75g (1 cup) desiccated coconut
½ tsp Himalayan salt
85g (¼ cup) maple syrup
1 tbsp maca powder

For the filling
2 apples, peeled,
    cored and diced
2 tbsp coconut sugar
1 tbsp lemon juice
½ tsp ground cinnamon

For the toffee sauce
125g (1 cup) pitted dates,
    soaked for 30 minutes
    or until very soft
3 tbsp almond milk
2 tbsp maple syrup
generous pinch of
    Himalayan salt
1 tbsp maca powder (optional)

For the nut crumble
50g (½ cup) pecans
65g (½ cup) cashews
35g (¼ cup) almonds

dairy-free ice cream, to serve
    (see our freezer recipes on
    pages 112–131)

SERVES 8—12

Line a 20cm pie tin with baking paper.

Start with the base. Place the cashews, desiccated coconut and salt in a high-powered food processor and blend on high until fine. Take out 3–4 tablespoons of the mixture and set aside in a bowl. Add the maple syrup to the food processor with the maca and a splash of water and blend until well combined and the mixture sticks together. Press into the pie tin, pressing it up the sides. Clean out the bowl of the food processor.

For the filling, place half the chopped apples into the clean food processor with the remaining filling ingredients and blend until roughly broken up into small pieces, then place into a bowl and stir in the rest of the apple chunks. Clean out the food processor bowl again.

Next, make the toffee sauce. Place the dates into the clean food processor with the remaining sauce ingredients and blend on high for 3–5 minutes until very smooth. Pour this mixture into the bowl with the apple filling and stir together. Pour into the pie base. Don't wash out your food processor – you'll need any toffee sauce left in it for the crumble.

For the nut crumble, pulse the nuts on high in the food processor until roughly broken up into large chunks – the mixture will stick together slightly. Spread the crumble on top of the apple filling, then sprinkle over the reserved base mixture. Place in the fridge for 1–2 hours to set, then serve chilled. Perfect with a scoop of one of our ice creams.

tarts, pies & pudding pots

Rhubarb & Raspberry Raw Crumble

Rhubarb is one of those vegetables (amazingly it is a vegetable and not a fruit) that we can't get enough of when it's in season. A Sunday without a crumble is a sad state of affairs and we're very proud of our take on this quintessentially English classic.

For the filling

200g (2 cups) rhubarb, cut into chunks

4 tbsp rice malt syrup or alternative liquid natural sweetener

3 tbsp coconut sugar

125g (1 cup) raspberries

60g (½ cup) pitted dates

½ tsp vanilla powder

For the crust

60g (½ cup) dates

80g (1 cup) walnuts

70g (½ cup) almonds

35g (½ cup) desiccated coconut

3 pinches of salt

1 tbsp maca powder

½ tsp ground cinnamon

2 tbsp rice malt syrup or alternative liquid natural sweetener

For the crumble topping

40g (½ cup) walnuts

50g (½ cup) pecans

25g (¼ cup) pistachios

30g (¼ cup) coconut sugar

35g (¼ cup) sunflower seeds

20g (½ cup) coconut flakes

½ tbsp rice malt syrup or alternative liquid natural sweetener (optional)

SERVES 8—12

Preheat the oven to no higher than 42°C or to its lowest temperature.

For the filling, mix the rhubarb with 2 tablespoons of the malt syrup and 2 tablespoons of the coconut sugar in a baking dish and bake for 3 hours. Meanwhile, toss the raspberries with the remaining coconut sugar and set aside. Once the rhubarb is dehydrated and soft, take it out of the oven and set aside.

For the crust, blend the dates and nuts in a high-powered food processor on high until fine. Add the remaining dry ingredients and blend again, adding the rice malt syrup at the end to help the mixture to stick together. If it's not sticky enough, add a few drops of water. Press the mixture into a 20cm round fluted pie tin, pushing it up the sides. Leave in the fridge for 2 hours to set. Clean out the bowl of the food processor.

For the crumble topping, blitz all the ingredients, except for the coconut flakes in the clean food processor, for a few seconds until the nuts are roughly broken up, keeping the mixture nice and chunky. Pour the crumble mixture into a bowl, add the coconut and mix by hand, adding the rice malt syrup, if needed, until it sticks together. Set aside.

To finish the filling, blend the dates to a paste then add the rhubarb. Add half the sugared raspberries, the remaining rice malt syrup and vanilla and blend briefly until just combined. Sweeten the mixture if desired. Stir in the remaining raspberries, pour the filling over the crust and scatter the crumble on top. Press the crumble down gently and chill for 1–2 hours to set.

163

Mango, Lime & Avocado Mousse Tart

This is a light, zesty torte in which you can really taste the freshness of the fruit. With the creamiest consistency created by using avocado, you won't believe how good this is until you've tried it. Uniquely palate-cleansing, it's the perfect treat to end a light summer dinner.

For the crust
130g (1 cup) macadamias
100g (1 cup) pecans
95g (¾ cup) pitted dates,
    soaked for 30 minutes
    or until soft
¼ tsp vanilla powder
pinch of salt

For the filling
3 small avocados, stoned
zest and juice of 1 lime
100g (½ cup) coconut oil
1 large mango, peeled
    and destoned
170g (½ cup) rice malt syrup
    or coconut syrup
pinch of Himalayan salt

164

SERVES 8—12

Line a 20cm round pie tin with baking paper.

First make the crust. Place the nuts in a high-powered food processor and blend on high until broken up. Add the remaining ingredients and blend again until well combined and the mixture sticks together. Press into the pie tin, and clean out the bowl of the food processor.

For the filling, blend the avocados in the clean food processor until smooth. Add the remaining ingredients and blend until everything has been broken down and the mixture is silky smooth. Pour over the base and place in the fridge for 2–3 hours to set.

Orange Chia Marmalade Parfait

We first created this when experimenting with desserts for a summer garden party we were throwing. Coconut cream and orange make for a deliciously light, fluffy texture – complete with layers of marmalade and crumble. It was a hit, providing equal measures of refreshment and indulgence.

For the orange chia marmalade

1 orange

1 tbsp rice malt syrup
   or maple syrup

3 tbsp chia seeds

For the orange cream

2 x 400ml cans coconut milk
   (place in the fridge
   overnight, only use the
   top layer of cream)

zest 1 orange and 3 tbsp juice

1 tbsp rice malt syrup
or maple syrup

For the marinated oranges

1 orange, peeled and segmented

2 tbsp orange juice

2 tbsp coconut sugar

For the crumble

25g (¼ cup) pecans

35g (¼ cup) almonds

30g (¼ cup) Brazil nuts

30g (¼ cup) coconut sugar

1 tbsp maca powder (optional)

MAKES 3 SMALL GLASS RAMEKINS OR JARS

First make the chia marmalade. Grate the orange zest into a bowl, then peel the orange. Blend the segments in a high-powered food processor for just a few seconds to break them down into rough pulp. Add to the zest and add in the syrup and chia seeds. Mix in well and leave in the fridge for 30–40 minutes or until the chia seeds have swelled and the mixture has a jam-like consistency. If you find it's still too runny, add another tablespoon of chia seeds and place back in the fridge. Clean out the bowl of the food processor.

For the cream, scoop out the layer of cream on the top of the watery coconut milk and add to the clean food processor with the orange zest, juice and syrup and blend for just a few seconds until well combined and creamy – try not to over-mix this. Transfer to a bowl and place in the fridge to firm up.

For the marinated oranges, cut the orange segments into chunks (around 3 chunks per segment). Place in a bowl with the juice and coconut sugar and mix together well. Set to one side until you are ready to assemble the parfait.

For the crumble, place all the ingredients into the clean food processor and blend on high just until the nuts are roughly chopped – keep this nice and chunky for some bite.

To assemble, use a small glass or ramekin and layer in the crumble, oranges, cream, chia marmalade, cream and so on, sprinkling some crumble on top to finish.

165

Avocado Cacao Ganache

The avocado ganache is a bit of a classic in the world of raw desserts. Often the one that people choose to achieve that 'OMG I can't believe it's not butter' reaction from first-timers. It has to be said that there's something pretty impressive about the transformation of the savoury snack to sweet, silky cream at the push of a button.

For the ganache
3 pitted Medjool dates
1½ medium avocados, stoned
40g (½ cup) cacao powder
110g (⅓ cup) rice malt syrup
  or maple syrup
30g (¼ cup) coconut sugar
½ tsp vanilla powder
2 pinches of salt
1 tbsp maca powder (optional)
1 tbsp chaga powder (optional)

For the cacao crumble topping
25g (¼ cup) pecans
45g (¼ cup) raw buckwheat
30g (¼ cup) goji berries
30g (¼ cup) pitted
  Medjool dates
pinch of ground cinnamon
2 tbsp cacao powder
2 tbsp coconut sugar

MAKES 3 SMALL RAMEKINS

To make the ganache, place the dates in a high-powered food processor and blend on high, then add the avocados and blend to form a paste. Add all the remaining ingredients and keep blending until the mixture is nice and gooey. Set aside in a bowl while you make the crumble topping, and clean out the bowl of the food processor.

For the crumble, add the nuts, buckwheat and gojis to the clean food processor and blend on high until well combined. Add all the remaining ingredients and pulse until the mixutre is nice and crumbly. It shouldn't be wet.

Finally, assemble the ganache by layering ganache in the ramekins and finishing with a layer of crumble on top. Store in the fridge until ready to serve.

166

Passionfruit & Pomegranate Parfait

Because of its sweet, appealing pastel hues, we like to serve this in individual pots at dinner parties. The pomegranate seeds are the *pièce de résistance* here, with their crunchy texture and juicy flavours. Choose jars with screw lids if you want to keep the parfait in the fridge for later. If left in the fridge overnight, it will become like a potted cheesecake – double win. *(Pictured on page 121.)*

For the pomegranate layer

65g (½ cup) cashews,
  soaked for 1 hour
  then drained
60ml (¼ cup) coconut milk
80g (½ cup) fresh pomegranate
  seeds, plus extra to decorate
2 tbsp coconut syrup
  or rice malt syrup
¼ tsp vanilla powder

For the passionfruit layer

65g (½ cup) cashews,
  soaked for 1 hour
  then drained
60ml (¼ cup) coconut milk
2 passionfruits, seeds only,
  plus extra to decorate
2 tbsp coconut syrup
  or rice malt syrup

MAKES 3–4 SMALL POTS

Place all the ingredients for the pomegranate layer in a high-powered blender and blend on high until completely smooth. Pour into small jars or glass ramekins, topping with some extra pomegranate seeds, and place in the fridge to set. Clean out the blender.

In the clean blender, add all the ingredients for the passionfruit layer. Blend on high until smooth then pour the mixture on top of the pomegranate layer.

Top with extra passionfruit seeds and pomegranate seeds. Put in the fridge for 1–2 hours to set, and enjoy chilled.

167

Coconut, Pistachio & Ginger Whip

Pistachio is one of our all-time favourite flavours. It's so delicate and combining it with ginger gives it that extra sparkle. A light, whipped cream dream you won't be able to put down, these subtle flavours keep you coming back for more.

2 x 400ml cans full-fat coconut milk (place in the fridge overnight, then only use the top layer of cream)

3 tbsp rice malt syrup or maple syrup

25g (¼ cup) pistachios

1 tbsp ground ginger

SERVES 2

Scoop out the layer of cream on the top of the watery coconut milk and add it to a high-powered blender or food processor then whip until soft – don't overdo this. Transfer to a bowl and clean out the bowl of the blender or food processor.

Add the malt syrup or maple syrup and pistachios to the clean food processor or blender and blend very briefly on high until the nuts are broken up and nicely incorporated, but still very chunky. Transfer to the bowl with the whipped coconut cream and fold in the ginger gently.

To serve, spoon into two small ramekins or jars as a tasty ice cream alternative, or use this cream as a side to a pie or berry dessert.

169

Crushed Berry Trifle

This is a raw dessert Grandma would be proud of. Layers of rich, British flavours come together to form this towering superfood trifle.

For the chia berry mix
250g (2 cups) mixed berries: strawberries, blueberries, blackberries, raspberries, plus extra for layering
2 tbsp rice malt syrup or alternative liquid natural sweetener
4 tbsp chia seeds

For the crumble layer
40g (½ cup) walnuts
50g (½ cup) pecans
45g (¼ cup) raw buckwheat
30g (¼ cup) coconut sugar
2 tbsp rice malt syrup or alternative liquid natural sweetener
pinch of salt

For the vanilla cream layer
65g (½ cup) macadamias, soaked for 1–2 hours
65g (½ cup) cashews, soaked for 1–2 hours
110g (⅓ cup) rice malt syrup or alternative liquid natural sweetener
125ml (½ cup) filtered water
3 tbsp coconut oil, melted
2 tbsp almond milk
1 tsp vanilla powder
1 tsp ground cinnamon

SERVES 3—4

To make the chia berry mix, place the berries in a high-powered food processor and blend on high for a few seconds only, so that they are still chunky. Add the sweetener and whizz to combine. Transfer the mixture to a bowl and add the chia seeds, stir in well and place in the fridge for 1 hour to set. Clean out the bowl of the food processor.

For the crumble layer, add all the ingredients to the clean food processor and blend roughly until still chunky. Set aside in a bowl.

Place the nuts for the vanilla cream layer in a high-speed blender and blend on high until ground, then add all the remaining ingredients until the mixture is thick and creamy. Place in the fridge for 2 hours until set or slightly firmer.

Assemble the trifle in either a large trifle bowl or 3–4 glasses or tall ramekins. Add a layer of crumble, then fresh berries, followed by the vanilla cream then a layer of the chia berry mix, repeat until your glasses or the trifle bowl are full to the brim, finishing with a crumble layer and more fresh berries.

tarts, pies & pudding pots

raw cake

Strawberry & Ginger Eton Mess

A traditional Eton mess should be the eighth wonder of the world – a scrumptious melting pot of naughtiness. Creating this raw version was one of our biggest recipe challenges yet: no matter how much we tried, we just couldn't get it as good as the original. A breakthrough moment came just as we were handing over the recipes for this book and we absolutely couldn't leave it out!

For the meringues

1 x 400g can chickpeas, drained, water reserved and chickpeas set aside for another day
3 tbsp rice malt syrup
60ml (¼ cup) lemon juice
4 tbsp coconut sugar, ground in a blender until fine

For the coconut cream

2 x 400ml cans coconut milk (place in the fridge overnight, then only use the top layer of cream)
1 tsp freshly grated ginger
½ tbsp lemon zest, plus extra to decorate
2 tbsp rice malt syrup
175g (¾ cup) strawberries, quartered, plus extra to serve
cornflower petals, to decorate

SERVES 2

Preheat the oven to no higher than 42°C or to its lowest temperature.

For the meringues, pour the chickpea water, syrup and lemon juice into a large bowl and whisk with an electric whisk for 5–7 minutes, adding the coconut sugar 1 tablespoon at a time. Keep whisking until the mixture thickens and forms stiff peaks. Pour the mixture onto a baking paper- or foil-lined baking sheet and place in the oven to dehydrate for 3–4 hours. Keep an eye on it as you don't want it to dry out too much or it will become sticky. When the mixture is dry to the touch and the edges can be cracked off, it is ready to take out and break into chunks.

To make the coconut cream, scoop out the layer of cream on the top of the coconut milk, and place in a high-powered food processor with the ginger, lemon zest and rice malt syrup. Blend or pulse gently for a few seconds until the mixture breaks down and becomes like whipped cream. Add to a mixing bowl with the strawberries and fold together.

To assemble, divide the cream/strawberry mixture between two bowls or ramekins. Crumble in a few meringue pieces and fill to the top with more cream mixture, finishing off with more crumbled meringue and strawberry pieces. You can assemble this dessert before a dinner or party and leave in the fridge for 1–2 hours until ready to serve, or eat immediately. Decorate with cornflower petals just before serving.

Strawberry Angel Whip

This is the non-powdered, natural sister of a 1970s' instant household favourite. If you weren't lucky enough to have Angel Delight the first time round, this will more than show you what you missed.

5-6 large fresh strawberries

2 x 400ml cans coconut milk (place in the fridge overnight, then only use the top layer of cream)

1 tbsp coconut syrup

SERVES 2

Place the strawberries into a high-powered food processor and blend on high until they are roughly broken up.

Scoop out the layer of cream on the top of the watery coconut milk, and add to the strawberries with the coconut syrup. Blend until everything is smooth and combined.

Place the mixture into a freezerproof container and transfer to the freezer for 20–30 minutes until it has set slightly, then transfer to two bowls or cups and serve straight away.

174

Coconut Cream
The thick layer of cream at the top of a can of coconut milk makes a great alternative to dairy cream in sweet dishes as well as savoury, and it's just as indulgent, rich and velvety-smooth as its dairy equivalent.

tarts, pies & pudding pots

Notes on Decorating & Styling

We're always in awe of how much difference the right decoration can make to the appearance of our raw creations. It really is the cherry on the cake, so to speak! We've had a lot of time to play around with our style and figure out what we think a cake by The Hardihood should look like. Of course, it's always changing based on the season or what we can get our hands on, but the idea is that the theme should run throughout. We like to think that if you had to pick a cake from a line-up, you'd know which one was ours.

Using other recipes as decoration
is a great way to enhance your cake.
Try brownie cubes or protein balls,
or save some of the base of a
cheesecake and roll it into mini balls
to use for toppers.

Celebration Cakes

Our favourite thing about being in the business of cake making is that we're in the business of celebrations. We love being a part of someone's happiest moment. We hear from so many people that The Hardihood cakes have contributed to their birthday, wedding, engagement, hen party, baby shower being a huge success, and it really reminds us why we do what we do. Cake always gets an invite to the party, and preparing food for yourself or for others is an expression of love.

When decorating your raw cake the sky is the limit. We've become known for our minimalist style, but if you want to go all out and throw a decoration party, go for it. You've done the hard part in making the cake and you can let the fun part take centre stage. Putting your own touch on your cake is a great outlet for your creativity. For us, no two cakes are ever the same, and that's what keeps it exciting.

First, look at the cake that you've made, look at the colours and the flavours and think about what might complement it best. Perhaps it would look great to match the decoration to the flavour, using raspberries to decorate a berry-flavoured dessert, or maybe some contrast is what it needs? Matching a bitter chocolate bark to a creamy sweet pie can offset the flavours wonderfully.

notes on decorating & styling

Use cashew cream (see page 80) to decorate your creation, using a piping bag. Practise swirls, lines or zig-zags etc., to find your favourite style. If you mess it up, you can simply scrape it off with the blunt side of a knife and try again.

Ideas for cake toppers and sprinklers

— fresh edible flowers
— dried edible flowers, including cornflower petals, rose petals or marigold petals
— desiccated or flaked coconut
— cacao nibs
— crushed nuts
— fresh herbs, as whole sprigs, picked leaves or chopped
— bee pollen (see note on safe use on p181)
— any type of edible seed
— goji berries or other dried berries
— fresh berries or fruits
— dehydrated fruits
— piped cashew creams, flavoured or plain
— cut-up pieces of raw cake or brownies
— chocolate sauce, drizzled on top
— chocolate bark

Styling your photo for social media

If you want to share your creations with others, it's really worth going the whole hog and not just decorating your dishes but thinking about how you present them.

When styling a raw cake or treat for an Instagram snap, it's important to remember that everything in the photo will be noticed. Be sure to clear a space on your worktop or table – an uncluttered image will show off your creation much better. A white background or surface is usually our preferred setting, but a sheet of coloured paper, a tea towel or a clean wooden table can look just as effective.

Lighting is key, so make sure you take your photo using as much natural light as possible – next to a window is ideal. If you're using your mobile, make use of filters or editing tools, experiment with them and find your favourite look. Your social media page will naturally start to look more cohesive if you use the same kind of editing techniques on every image.

KEEP ME COLD

Edible flowers are a game changer when it comes to decorating. They can make any dessert, breakfast or even a smoothie come alive. We love mixing them with herbs such as red amaranth for a luxurious, contemporary look.

notes on decorating & styling

Glossary
of Ingredients

Acai

Vibrant in colour, this ancient purple berry grows on the palms of the acai tree, commonly found in the rainforests of the Amazon. We use it in powdered form for its deep luxurious hues and pungent berry flavour. Rich in antioxidants, it helps keep cells strong and aids them in fighting the invasion of free radicals. It is also high in vitamin C, vital for a healthy immune system.

Adaptogens

Adaptogens are a unique group of herbal ingredients that support adrenal function and strengthen the body's response to stress. Working like a thermometer, they sense if things are heating up and so cool them down – and vice versa. Adaptogens need to be used regularly for a prolonged period of time before the effects can be noticed.

Almonds

Rumour has it that almonds are the most popular nut in the world, and it's easy to see why. Sweet in flavour and either creamy when soaked or packing a satisfying crunch when lightly crushed, almonds are incredibly versatile. Originally native to the Middle East, we tend to associate their milky flavour with marzipan or amaretto. They're particularly high in vitamin E, which protects cell membranes and keeps skin and hair glowing.

Apple Cider Vinegar

Apple cider vinegar comes from 'apple must', which is basically what is left when you crush an apple with stem, skin and seeds intact. During the oxygenation and fermentation process the sugars in the apple turn from alcohol and then to acetic acid, and this is what gives apple cider vinegar the health benefits it's known for. A great aid for digestion, it helps to kill pathogens, break up mucus in the body and clear the lymphatic system. Tangy and slightly moreish, it'll add a kick to any citrusy flavoured tonic.

Ashwagandha

Ashwagandha is an adaptogen from India and is, surprisingly, from the same family as the tomato. The root of the plant is dried and then powdered and used to tackle stress and anxiety as well as promoting relaxation and restoration. Add to an early evening brew to set you up for a good night's sleep or to a morning smoothie if you have a big day ahead.

Astragalus

Astragalus is an adaptogenic herb that comes from a type of bean or legume. It protects the body from physical, mental and emotional stress and is the main ingredient of a popular Chinese medicine called Huang Qi. It's a powerful chi tonic and is used to fight colds, flu and other respiratory infections.

Baobab

This African superfruit dries on the branch of the baobab tree, also known as the Tree of Life. The fruit is also rich in soluble fibre that helps maintain digestive regularity and may function as a prebiotic. It's also rich in vitamin C, which supports skin health and collagen production. We rely on it for its high level of antioxidants and love its tart, lemon-curd-like flavour.

Bee Pollen

Bee pollen is the primary source of protein used to build a bee hive. It is carried to the worker bees on the back of foraging bees where it is packed into pollen balls. Hugely nutritious, it is good for enhancing energy and soothing skin. It is worth noting that there's an ethical argument for not eating bee pollen as it was intended for growing the hive, and one teaspoon of it takes one working bee eight hours every day for a month to gather. NOTE: Bee pollen can provoke a severe reaction if you have a pollen allergy. Avoid if pregnant or breastfeeding, or if you are taking blood-thinning medication.

Buckwheat

Many mistake buckwheat for a grain when it's actually a fruit seed. It comes from the buckwheat flower and is related to rhubarb and sorrel. It is gluten- and wheat-free and full of trace minerals and vitamins. When eaten raw it has a satisfying crunch.

Brown Rice Syrup

Brown rice syrup comes from fermented brown rice in which the starch in the grains has been broken down. The liquid is removed and heated. Brown rice syrup is a natural sweetener but should be used sparingly.

Cacao Butter

Extracted from the cacao bean, cacao butter is a pale yellow vegetable fat with a chocolatey taste. It's used to make chocolate and is solid at room temperature, which is helpful in raw recipes. It's calorific, but responsible for giving chocolate that melt-in-your-mouth sensation.

Cacao Nibs

The cacao nib is what's left once the cacao bean that grows on the Theobroma cacao tree has been fermented, dried and roasted and the shells have been removed. Hugely nutritious and energy enhancing, they boast large quantities of copper, magnesium, zinc and iron. We love them for their bitter but nutty flavour and use them to add texture and crunch to recipes.

Cacao, Raw

Not to be confused with the more processed cacao, raw cacao comes from raw cacao pods that are sundried instead of roasted and then cold-pressed to separate the cacao from the cacao butter. It has a strong chocolate taste that smells divine but tastes bitter if unsweetened. It's a known heart-opener that may boost serotonin in the brain (this is known as the 'feel-good' chemical, because of its positive effect on mood and emotion). Cacao has long been used as a health elixir and as a ceremonial medicine; the Olmeca people used it as far back as 1900 BC, before it became a ritualistic medicine used by the Aztec and Mayan cultures.

Camu Camu

A small riverside-growing shrub found in the rainforests of the Amazon and Peru, Camu Camu is about the size of a lemon and is purple and orange in colour. It's full of vitamin C, has antiviral properties, strengthens the immune system and balances mood. We use it powdered in smoothies and creams.

Cashews

Native to the Amazon rainforest, cashews come from the bottom of the cashew apple. One of our favourite and most-used nuts, we get through an insane amount of cashews in our studio. Hugely versatile when soaked, they become buttery and creamy with a delicate flavour, or when used dry their spongy texture adds a soothing, warming quality to a cake.

Chaga

Chaga is a powerful medicinal mushroom that grows on living birch trees and takes 15–20 years to mature. It condenses many important nutrients and enzymes into a form that we can consume. High in antioxidants, this powerful adaptogenic improves immune response, promotes overall wellbeing and is a great source of caffeine-free energy.

Chia Seeds

These nutritious little seeds come from the *Salvia hispanica* plant, which is related to mint. Borrowed from the Aztecs, they are known for their energy-giving abilities. Translated literally, chia means strength in Mayan. Easy to digest, they swell to a frogspawn-like gel when soaked, creating a liquid that forms a nutritious base for puddings and potted desserts.

Chlorella Powder

Native to Taiwan and Japan, chlorella is the antioxidant-rich compound that gives plants their green colour. It improves circulation by increasing oxygen levels and encouraging cell rejuvination. It also contains magnesium and binds toxins and heavy metals, allowing them to be removed from the body.

Cinnamon

There are two different kinds of cinnamon; we use more of the cassia cinnamon which is powdered from the branches or bark of several trees. The other comes in neat rolls and tends to be used more in traditional cooking. A flavoursome sweetener with warming, soothing qualities, cinnamon can be used to create a sense of homeliness and is great in festive or autumnal desserts. It has been used as a Chinese medicine treatment for colds and joint pain and tests have given some support for its antibacterial and anti-inflammatory properties.

Coconut Nectar

Coconut nectar is probably our favourite sweetener because it needs no lengthy heat treatment to concentrate its flavour. It comes from the flower of the coconut palm and is dark in colour and extremely sweet, with not even a glimmer of coconut flavour.

Coconut Oil

Virgin, cold-pressed coconut oil is a staple in raw dessert making, as it's an extremely nutritious fat that can be found in the flesh of the coconut. It contains antimicrobial lipids that have antifungal, antibacterial and antiviral properties. It's primarily made up of medium-chain triglycerides that are easier for your body to digest and turn into energy. It's a rich alternative to butter or cream with a smooth texture. Coconut oil is solid at room temperature and turns to liquid if it is even a degree or two warmer. It is a staple in raw dessert making because of its versatility.

Coconut Sugar

Coconut sugar doesn't come from the actual coconut, but instead from the flower of the coconut palm. It begins life as coconut nectar before being dehydrated to form a mineral-rich powder. The texture of coconut sugar is quite coarse, but a few seconds in a high-powered blender will turn it into a fine dust reminiscent of icing sugar, which is great for fluffy creams and raw chocolate. Coconut sugar smells divine and has a rich, caramel flavour, which adds a lot to a dessert. It's low on the glycemic index and far more nutritious than any other powdered sugar, for sure.

Cold-Brew Coffee
Making cold-brew coffee is deceptively simple – it is made just by replacing heat with time. In this raw process, coffee beans are cold-water brewed for between 18 and 24 hours. While the flavour compounds and some caffeine from the beans are extracted, the bitter oils and fatty acids are left behind, making it smoother, more alkaline and easily bottled and transported.

Cordyceps
Cordyceps is a healthy fungus with a fascinating back story, known for improving drive, endurance and confidence. Traditionally it could only be formed when a caterpillar became infected with cordyceps spores, and the fungus would then consume the entire caterpillar until all that was left was a caterpillar-shaped mushroom. These days scientists know how to cultivate cordyceps in a laboratory.

Dates
Another crucial component to raw baking, dates are sticky, sweet and hugely versatile. Grown on the date palm, they dry on the branch before being gathered by hand and sorted for quality. They're rich in many vital nutrients and are one of the sweetest fruits. We use dates as a binding agent in a lot of our desserts, soaking them depending on how soft they are already. Make sure the dates you're choosing haven't been preserved with sulphites and be sure to remove the stones where possible; this is particularly easy to do once they've

been soaked. Rich in flavour, they taste like a luxurious caramel.

Desiccated Coconut
Brilliantly white and boasting all the health benefits of coconut, desiccated coconut is the grated, unsweetened fresh meat of the coconut that has been dried. It's inexpensive and its almost pearlescent glow is perfect for frostings, decoration and adding texture to protein balls or cake bases.

Echinacea
Most people know echinacea for its cold-fighting reputation, but it can also be used as a daily immunity booster and a painkiller. Made from a mix of active substances, several species of the plant are used to make supplements, from its flowers, leaves and roots. We add it to morning tonics to support and uplift throughout the day.

Filtered Water
When you're going to the effort of making sure that the ingredients you use are close to nature, it make sense to apply the same logic to the water you drink. Although we're hugely lucky to be in the 90 per cent of the world's population who have access to clean water, it's worth noting that the tap water we drink contains potentially harmful contaminants, pesticides and hormones. The ideal solution is to have a filtration system fitted in your house, but failing that a Brita filter is the second-best option.

Ginger
Fresh ginger is a seriously flavoursome ingredient and surprisingly fruitful when juiced. It is the underground rhizome or root of the ginger plant. It has a firm, fibrous texture and a little goes a long way. It's known for its

anti-inflammatory, immunity-enhancing qualities and is great for settling an upset stomach. We also find it helps clear the sinuses in the winter months. Use it to add spice and zing to juices, protein balls and recipes in which you'd rather not use too much added sweetener.

Ginseng

There are 11 different varieties of ginseng, all of which are characterized by their slow-growing, fleshy roots. Some places sell the ginseng root whole, and although this is a great way to check the quality it's much easier for your body to digest the powdered version. Ginseng is said to improve brain function, thinking and cognition. Traditional medical practitioners also recommend it for lowering stress levels and improving physical and mental energy.

Goji Berries

Goji berries can be bought as a juice or as a dried fruit, they're beautifully bright in colour and have a sweet but mellow flavour. Native to the Himalayan mountains of Tibet, they're said to be anti-inflammatory, antibacterial and antifungal. They've been used in Chinese medicine for 6,000 years, but are now readily available in most supermarkets. When soaked they swell to almost double their size. We use them decoratively or in pudding pots.

Hazelnuts

Hazelnuts are one of the most expensive nuts out there and for that reason they're a bit of a special-occasion nut for us. Synonymous with autumnal flavours and Nutella, the pale kernels are packed full of healthy oils, vitamin E and minerals. With a luxuriously rich, chocolatey flavour, they can be used to raise the quality of any dish, sweet or savoury.

Hemp Seeds

Typically found in the Northern Hemisphere, hemp comes from a variation of the cannabis plant. Not to be confused with its naughty sibling, hemp seeds are packed with minerals that help to rebuild and repair cells in the body. A fantastic source of protein, hemp seeds can also be bought in powder form, which is a great addition to raw desserts. With a mild, nutty flavour and as a great source of essential fatty acids, we use hemp powder if we feel we need grounding.

Himalayan Salt

Harbouring 84 of the same trace minerals and elements in the same proportions that can be found in the human body, Himalayan salt is known to stimulate circulation, lower blood pressure and remove heavy metals from the blood. We add a pinch to pretty much everything; it adds depth and contrast and always makes desserts tastier.

Lemon

Steadfast staples in our morning routines, lemons are rich in vitamin C and rejuvenate and uplift from within. A great blood purifier, antiseptic and alkalizer, lemons cleanse the digestive tract as they draw out toxins and support the immune system.

Linseed

Golden linseeds (also known as flax seeds) come from the flax plant, which grows in cooler climates, and although they can be found split or as an oil we prefer to work with the powdered version for optimum absorption. Powerhouses of nutrition, linseeds are one of the richest known plant sources of omega-3 fats that are essential for brain development and promote heart and joint health. They're also known as nature's answer to hormone replacement therapy and can be used to balance oestrogen levels, particularly for women going through the menopause.

Lucuma

Lucuma comes from the Peruvian lucuma fruit that looks like a cross between a mango and an avocado in its unpowdered form. A source of antioxidants, minerals and fibre as well as healthy carbohydrates, we love it for its maple-flavoured sweetness. In fact, in Peru lucuma is actually the most popular flavour of ice cream because it is so delicious.

Maca

Maca is one of our favourite superfood powders; it smells incredible and tastes smooth and creamy. Native to the Andes Mountains and part of the broccoli and watercress family, maca actually looks like a robust radish in its natural state. The Incas and Peruvians called it the food of gods because of its energy-giving abilities. It's said to be great for migraines, fertility and sex drive. With a subtle sweetness and malty fudge-like flavour, you can sprinkle maca on top of pretty much anything to make it taste creamier.

Macadamias

Macadamia nuts are native to Queensland, Australia, where they grow near streams. With similar qualities to cashews, these nuts are a great substitute for those who are cashew sensitive; they're both soft and absorbent with a mild, delicate flavour.

Maple Syrup

Maple syrup comes from the maple tree, which is most prevalent in Canada. A hole is drilled into the tree in springtime ('sugaring season') and the sugar-circulating fluid – or sap – drips out, which is harvested, taken to a 'sugar house' and then boiled until the water evaporates, leaving behind the rich, sweet syrup, which is then filtered.

Matcha

This bright green powder comes from Japanese tea leaves that are grown in the shade to increase chlorophyll content and are then hand-picked before being dried and ground. We've found matcha to be a bit of a Marmite character when it comes to flavour: some love it, others hate it. However, we're big fans and even though we know it's expensive we can't help but use it unsparingly. It is rich in antioxidants and has a concentrated caffeine kick.

Pearl Powder

Literally powder made from crushed pearls, pearl powder dates back to ancient Chinese skincare and medicine. A powerful antioxidant, it contains signal proteins that stimulate the regeneration of collagen. As you'd expect, it's pretty pricey, but it is one of those super-special purchases if you stumble across it.

Pecans

The pecan nut originates from central and eastern North America and the river valleys of Mexico and is from the same family as the walnut. Pecans are characteristically sweet in flavour and smooth in texture.

Pistachios

Another luxurious nut, pistachio is popular not only for its succulent, sweet flavour, but also for its desirable colour palette. We love its washed-out, pastel hues as much as we love its soft-mouth feel. A member of the cashew family, we use dehulled pistachios for easy access.

Probiotic Powder

This is a powdered dose of natural, live, good bacteria that helps promote gut health and prevent some associated ailments. When digestive flora is in check, we feel happier and lighter and energy that would otherwise be spent supporting digestion is free to assist with the other functions of the body, such as detoxification and healing. Make sure you use a good-quality probiotic. Some poorer-quality products may contain dead rather than live bacteria that will not survive passage through the stomach environment. Look for brands that are stored in the fridge and have a high strength of live, active cultures.

Pumpkin Seeds

Most people are quite familiar with pumpkin seeds, but perhaps not so familiar with their range of benefits. With a chewy texture and mellow flavour, pumpkin seeds are a valuable source of magnesium and omega-3, which promotes restful sleep.

Reishi

Reishi is another medicinal mushroom and is one of the most powerful adaptogens out there. It gets the immune system to work more effectively rather than blindly stimulating it. Some champion it for its meditative qualities, promoting calmness and balance within the body.

Schisandra

Native to northeast China and parts of Russia, the schisandra berry grows on a climbing vine. Used widely in beauty products because of its reputation for skin-protecting qualities, it's also thought to be particularly beneficial to kidney, lung and liver function. It has a sweet and tangy taste and complements strawberry flavours well.

Sprouted Chickpeas

Chickpeas can be used raw and sprouted, or if time is short, from a tin. To sprout chickpeas, soak the dried peas in filtered cold water and leave overnight, then drain and rinse thoroughly. Spread out on a baking tray, cover with a tea towel, and leave for at least 12 hours to sprout. They're a brilliant source of protein and magnesium and have a fulfilling texture when ground.

Sprouted Oats

The difference between sprouted oats and ordinary breakfast oats is in the production process. Normally oats are steamed before being rolled, but sprouted oats are simply soaked to unlock the nutrients, slowly dried and then rolled to retain more flavour and nutritional value.

Tahini

Tahini paste is made from sesame seeds that have been ground to a butter, thus releasing their oils and flavours. It's high in vitamins and minerals and lighter on the palate than nut butters. We use it in cake bases and balls for a savoury touch.

Tulsi

Tulsi is such an all-round performer that it's been labelled the Queen of Herbs; it's known to sharpen memory and promote the removal of mucus from the bronchial tube. It can be used to treat the common cold, flu, sore throats and chesty coughs as well as balance moods. Both the leaves and the seed of the plant are equally valuable. We prefer it in its powdered form, added to smoothies, teas and desserts. It is sweet in flavour and reminiscent of mint liquorice and Earl Grey tea.

Turmeric

We love turmeric – a knobbly root vegetable famous for its bright yellow colour and incredible anti-inflammatory qualities. We use it juiced or powdered at the onset of a sniffle and we also find it alleviates joint pain. Its citrusy, spicy flavours work well with lemon and ginger and it makes the best natural food colouring. Be careful, though, turmeric stains anything and everything it touches.

Vanilla

The vanilla pod grows alongside fragrant flowers on the tropical climbing orchid. Once picked it is ground down to a powder and sold as the second most expensive spice in the world after saffron. This heartwarming, luxurious flavour doesn't get enough credit in our opinion; there's nothing plain about the beautifully, homely notes of vanilla. We use it in everything, from our cheesecakes and mousses to chocolate-flavoured treats, and we prefer the powder to the more processed liquid version.

Walnuts

After almonds, walnuts are said to be the second most popular nut in the world. They grow inside kernels on the juglans tree and are thought to be particularly good for brain health, giving fuel to the argument that food resembles the organs it benefits. This is partly because walnuts contain a unique concoction of powerful antioxidants. Check the quality of walnuts before buying them, and steer clear of those that look shrivelled. They're one of the more perishable nuts and can quickly lose their lustre.

Spirulina

Rumour has it that spirulina is one of the oldest life forms on Earth. It's basically an edible powdered algae that grows in salt-water lakes in Africa and Mexico, which uses light, warmth, water and minerals to produce protein, carbohydrates, vitamins and other vital nutrients. Spirulina is reputed to be good for a whole host of serious conditions, including heart disease, cancer, high cholesterol, high blood pressure, anaemia and raised blood sugar levels. We love it for its deep velvety green colour and smooth, savoury flavour. In some smoothies we find it tastes like candy, but maybe we've just been doing this for too long.

Wheatgrass

Wheatgrass comes from the young shoot of the wheat plant. Full of chlorophyll, vitamins and nutrients that help protect the cells from oxidative stress, it's reputed to have a positive effect on digestion, the formation of red blood cells and restoring pH balance. Its mild, pale, lime green colour can be used as a natural food colouring as its flavour isn't overpowering.

Index

188

190

191

192

ACKNOWLEDGEMENTS

THANKS TO:

Dom Chung for the "in"

Danielle, Marina, Ellen and Lydia for helping with the leftovers

Ingrid for the man-hours

Jeremy for the storytelling and (mostly) good advice

Cathryn for imagining this book before we could

Mads for the guinea pig duty

Charlotte, Lizzie, Jemima and Amber for the art

Jones & Sons for being the savoury to our sweet

And the rest of our friends and family who've put up with us
talking about nothing but cake since 2014 — we couldn't have done
this without your unwavering support and enthusiasm.

The universe, for always having our backs.